ADVANCE PRAISE FOR *GOING OVER THE MOUNTAIN*

"*Going Over the Mountain* is a gorgeous tale of finding strength—and peace—in the mountains, and of raising girls to do the same. It's a reflection on entering the woods as a follower, a solo traveler, a parent, and in community, for anyone who's turned to the trail for comfort, or dreams of trying someday."
—Blair Braverman, adventurer and author of *Welcome to the Goddamn Ice Cube: Chasing Fear and Finding Home in the Great White North*

"In *Going Over the Mountain*, Christine Woodside evocatively weaves vignettes from her intrepid decades on the trail—as a young woman finding her footing, then as a mother leading her daughters, and, finally, as a solo hiker aware of her own strength. In unspooling the lessons she's learned from the mountains, Woodside offers an inspiring story about finding one's way, both as a woman and in the wilderness. This book will make you want to cancel your week plans and pack your backpack."
—Erica Berry, author of *Wolfish: Wolf, Self, and the Stories We Tell About Fear*

"With strong writing and a stack of true and compelling episodes, Christine Woodside takes her readers along on the progress of her mountain life from teen, to wife, to mother, and the liberating triumph of her one-on-one solos. This deeply insightful memoir is wise and funny, easy to pick up, and impossible to put down."
—Laura Waterman, climber and author of *Losing the Garden: The Story of a Marriage*

"I knew from her columns in *Appalachia* that Christine Woodside used word-magic, and here she uses it in a longer forum. Whether she is writing about her love for an old cooking pot or for camping in a storm with her daughters, reading T. S. Eliot poetry on the Appalachian Trail or racing to climb each New England state's highest mountain in 48 hours, her life among the mountains reminds us eloquently that life devoted to these places will save us."
—Elissa Ely, writer for the *Boston Globe*, WBUR, and *Appalachia*

T0245843

GOING OVER THE MOUNTAIN

One Woman's Journey from Follower
to Solo Hiker and Back

CHRISTINE WOODSIDE

Appalachian Mountain Club Books
Boston, Massachusetts

AMC is a nonprofit organization, and sales of AMC Books fund our mission of protecting the Northeast outdoors. If you appreciate our efforts and would like to become a member or make a donation to AMC, visit outdoors.org, call 603-466-2727, or contact us at Appalachian Mountain Club, 10 City Square, Boston, MA 02129.

outdoors.org/books-maps

Distributed by National Book Network
Cover design by Jon Lavalley © Appalachian Mountain Club
Interior photographs by Christine Woodside, unless otherwise noted
Photograph on page 162 © 2004 ScenicNH Photography LLC/Erin Paul Donovan. Used by permission.
Map "The All-Girl Quest" by Abigail Coyle © Appalachian Mountain Club

All or portions of "The Ramsey Trail," "The Battered Pot," "Eight Legs," "'Echo, Echo,'" "The Dead Horse," "What Lurks Beneath the Voice of Calm?," "Alone with the Alone," "Encounter with a Hare, " "*Really* Going Over the Mountain," "Human Nature on the Herd Path," "Straight Up," "Memory Fails, Loss Magnifies," "The Death of Geraldine Largay," and "Healing by Doing" were first published in *Appalachia*, the journal of the Appalachian Mountain Club.

"Rage on Grassy Ridge" was first published in the anthology *Soul of the Sky* (Mount Washington Press, 1999).

"My Secret Ledge" was first published in *Estuary* magazine, Fall 2020.

"Mama Bear to Baby Bear: Get Up That Tree *Now*" was adapted from a monologue performed for a Connecticut Forest and Park Association story event.

Published by the Appalachian Mountain Club. No part of this publication may be reproduced or transmitted in any form or by any means, electronic or mechanical, including photocopying and recording, or by any information storage or retrieval system, except as may be expressly permitted by the 1976 Copyright Act or in writing from the publisher.

Library of Congress Cataloging-in-Publication Data
Names: Woodside, Christine, 1959- author.
Title: Going over the mountain : one woman's journey from follower to solo hiker and back / Christine Woodside.
Description: Boston, Massachusetts : Appalachian Mountain Club Books, [2023] | Summary: "Going Over the Mountain charts the course of author Christine Woodside's outdoors journey-alone, with friends, and especially with her daughters-with insight, humor, and an abiding love for the outdoors"-- Provided by publisher.
Identifiers: LCCN 2023020269 (print) | LCCN 2023020270 (ebook) | ISBN 9781628421521 (trade paperback : alk. paper) | ISBN 9781628420852 (epub) | ISBN 9781628420869 (mobi)
Subjects: LCSH: Woodside, Christine, 1959- | Women hikers--United States--Biography. | Women travelers--United States--Biography. | Hiking for women.
Classification: LCC GV191.52.W665 A3 2023 (print) | LCC GV191.52.W665 (ebook) | DDC 796.51092 [B]--dc23/eng/20230522
LC record available at https://lccn.loc.gov/2023020269
LC ebook record available at https://lccn.loc.gov/2023020270

The paper used in this publication meets the minimum requirements of the American National Standard for Information Sciences-Permanence of Paper for Printed Library Materials, ANSI Z39.48-1984. ∞

Outdoor recreation activities by their very nature are potentially hazardous. This book is not a substitute for good personal judgment and training in outdoor skills. Due to changes in conditions, use of the information in this book is at the sole risk of the user. The authors and the Appalachian Mountain Club assume no liability for accidents happening to, or injuries sustained by, readers who engage in the activities described in this book.

Interior pages and cover are printed on responsibly harvested paper stock certified by The Forest Stewardship Council®, an independent auditor of responsible forestry practices.

Printed in the United States of America, using vegetable-based inks.

5 4 3 2 1   23 24 25 26 27 28 29 30

For my daughters, Elizabeth and Annie,
who believed we would see Grassy Ridge

CONTENTS

Part I: Bonded

Part II: The Girls

Part III: Alone

Part IV: Forward

Part I

BONDED

Nudged Upward

I climbed my first mountain in lime-green cotton pants that kept slipping down and releasing the hem of my white shirt.

I was 3. I wore blue sneakers and followed my family upward on the Pasture Trail, pushing through high grasses and squinting in the July sun. My parents and older brothers trudged ahead of me through the steep field. Bob, Steve, and John were big boys: 9, 8, and 6 years old. My father told me I would like this mountain because it had a wonderful view at the top. My mother carried a picnic in a rectangular basket with handles. The grass stood tall, up to my waist, and that pasture glinted in the bright sun. We inched upward. This was so hard. I panted. I stopped. Mommy waited for me and then nudged me along. I did not like this.

Standing by a red pine on Rattlesnake Mountain, Holderness, New Hampshire, 1962. *Gloria Woodside*

Mommy and I hiked by ourselves because I could not keep up. I heard my brothers' yells. Exciting things were happening ahead. My mother cajoled me in her soft voice, "Come on, Chrissie! We will eat lunch on the top." It seemed very far off to me. Step. Step. Stumble.

Eventually the Pasture Trail entered a fringe of small oaks and red pines with their brittle, blocky bark. Mommy and I stepped between giant rocks. I then stumbled onto a large, rocky open area overlooking the sparkling lake.

We were not supposed to go to the cliff edge. My brothers kept running over there anyway and looking down. I did not walk out to the cliff. I just took one step onto the big, flat rock and then ran back the other way. My mother kept calling to the boys, "Away from the edge!"

Mommy had a camera and asked me to stand by a red pine at the fringe of woods back from the ledge. She tucked my shirt in, stepped back, pointed the camera, and said, "You climbed the mountain!" My face was flushed and I looked off to my right instead of at the lens. I was not smiling. That had been hard.

These first-year photos captured a girl who was not sure what to do surrounded by rooty paths, giant rocks, and enormous pines. In another picture she asked me to sit on a large rock near the lake, by another red pine. "Hold out your purse and show us, Chrissie." I frowned but held it very high for her. Why not?

My three brothers, Daddy, Mommy, and I all perched on the outcropping, eating peanut butter and jelly sandwiches. Then Daddy said we should all sit around Mommy with the water, fuzzy treetops, and the distant dark-blue hills behind us. He took a picture.

Memories of this day have come back to me in bits over the years. My father placed the photo inside a paperweight he used at his office. This was my family's mountain origin story, on West Rattlesnake Mountain cliffs, 1,230 feet above sea level, overlooking Squam Lake in central New Hampshire.

With my purse, Squam Lake, New Hampshire, 1962.
Christine Woodside archive

That was the day I learned to love the top. Going down was easy. My brothers ran, grabbing trees and swinging down into the grassy hill. I minced cautiously, but I was laughing now.

THE SHORTCUT

One day shortly before I turned 7 years old, I looked out the glass doors in the back of our kitchen and saw an unfamiliar boy walking through our yard. I called to my mother, "What's he doing?"

Oh, he's taking a shortcut," she said. We lived on a corner, and he was saving himself a little time. She seemed totally unconcerned that he was trespassing. Most of the families knew each other in the Riverside Drive neighborhood of Princeton, New Jersey, but many people's yards had fences or bushes around them, and it was unusual to see people cutting through. I was shocked, and intrigued, that this kid cut through our yard to take an alternate route.

I became obsessed with finding alternate routes. I enlisted my friend Frances, who was in my first-grade class. I asked her if she thought we could find a shortcut to school. She thought we could.

The problem was that I lived basically across the street from Riverside School. I could see the building from our front yard. Frances lived several streets away, and lately I'd been walking down to meet her on weekday mornings before walking back past my house and on to school with her.

We looked for a shortcut from Frances's house to where

Two of my brothers in our back yard, with the side street visible at the back, 1963. *Christine Woodside archive*

she met me. We tried looping around another road and back around to mine, but this route seemed to take much longer.

One gray morning in late winter, Frances was waiting for me at the corner of Sycamore Road. She waved and beckoned. "I found a shortcut!"

"You did?" I asked.

"Well, it's sort of a stupid one," she said.

She turned onto Sycamore, and I followed her to a long hedge. In spring this hedge bloomed yellow, but now it was just a gray assemblage of branches. Frances leaned down and stepped in; I stayed close behind. She started pushing through the hedge, leading me along a grotto of sticks. Sometimes I had to shove back the stiff branches before they poked me in the eye. I kept as close to Frances's back as I could. Crouching, we crashed our way through the hedge. It seemed that we would never reach the end.

Eventually, I saw daylight around Frances. We were almost to an opening. She climbed out, and I stumbled behind. We stood up on the grass. We blinked. We were at the corner of my road and Sycamore Road.

We'd done it. It was kind of silly, but it was our adventure. The very air looked different.

GRANDMOM AND MOM

My grandmother leaned over the toilet in the upstairs bathroom of her house at the shore. She held tight the plastic toilet brush and swished it fast around the bowl while talking to me:

"Granddad was never sick a day in his life until now." She flushed the toilet and tapped the lid down. "And now I've got this big house to take care of, and him too."

Granddad was a tall, strong, funny man. He used to imitate a trombone with his voice and fingers. He called Coca-Cola "cola-coca." But lately he was quiet. He had heart disease. At the age of 7, I had never considered what it could mean never to be sick a day in your life. I was sick a few times a year. Sometimes I got stomach bugs, usually around my birthday in March. I caught colds. I felt nauseous even on a short car ride.

Not Granddad. He'd always been healthy until now. Grandmom was complaining about her life to me, which made me feel trusted. But I knew she could handle it all, even though that house did seem very big. It held bedrooms for me, my three brothers, my parents, and even a visiting cousin or two. That week, my brother John and I were there without our older brothers or parents. It was a special

I'm third from left, standing with some of my large extended family, Ocean City, New Jersey, 1967. My grandmother stands second from right, my father third from right, and my mother fifth from right. *Christine Woodside archive*

visit for us. While Grandmom cleaned, I followed her around like a domestic disciple.

My grandparents lived on a curvy street in Ocean City, New Jersey. Stucco covered the house's outside walls, and a balcony opened off the upstairs living room. The house seemed like two dwellings, one on top of the other. Downstairs, a large kitchen with a big table occupied one side of the house. On the other side, a small hallway led to three or four bedrooms, which Grandmom had decorated with white Formica furniture and colored accents. I liked the pink room, but I also had slept in the blue and yellow rooms. Upstairs, a sofa, comfortable chairs, and a television lined the edges of the carpeted living room, one side of which led to the balcony. Tucked behind the sofa wall stood a galley kitchen. At breakfast, Grandmom would sit me down at the tiny table and let me choose from her collection of single-serving boxes of cereal. They reminded me of doll's food. I loved them.

My grandparents' saltshakers had insulated lids. You pressed them with your thumb and they creaked open. I could see, through the clear plastic, grains of rice mixed in with the salt. Grandmom said that was to absorb moisture, water that went through the air and that no one could see. She said everyone at the shore had to add rice to their saltshakers, or the salt would not pour. Everything, just everything, down at the shore was damp, according to Grandmom. I didn't notice the damp at the beach where we swam and dug in the sand for hours; where I knew how to vault myself into the wave and catch it just at the right second and ride it in; where I didn't care if the sand went into my bathing suit. Freedom.

From the house's balcony, we could look west, away from the ocean, toward the bay that separated the island of Ocean City from the rest of New Jersey, including my house, a 2-hour drive away.

Grandmom stood about 4 foot 11 inches tall. She wore little flat shoes and cotton dresses with an apron on top. In the evening, she gave Granddad his dinner first: a sandwich and soup that he ate on a TV tray while watching the television news from 6 feet away (for safety from radiation, they said). But Grandmom sat closer to the TV, and she smoked Tareyton cigarettes and leafed through *TV Guide* to find when *Jeopardy* and *Hollywood Squares* would air. I would perch near her, listening to her stories of all the cousins, whose pictures peered out at us from a standing flip-book. Grandmom was a woman who knew who she was inside that house.

Step outside the house, and Grandmom was not in command. In the garage stood one car: Grandad's Cadillac. Grandmom did not know how to drive it, or any car, because she had never learned. My grandfather did not think women should drive. His reason was that women were not good drivers. My mother and her two sisters, my aunts, never drove until they got married. Grandmom had lived in Philadelphia most of her life and so must have taken buses and the elevated train. When she and Granddad retired to Ocean City, she needed rides everywhere. She depended on Granddad to take her to the grocery store and to church, as well as other places. She could not go anywhere without her husband's consent and help.

I never thought about how limited her movement in the world really was until Granddad died of a heart attack a few years after being diagnosed with heart disease. He was 67. My father was helping with his estate, so we visited Grandmom at the shore to meet with her about the will. My first thought when my parents said we were going to see her was, "Yay!" But the entire mood there had changed. It was fall, and chilly. The light hit the stucco walls differently. The front lawn had gone to sandy weeds. We found Grandmom on her sofa in a melancholy state, which was so confusing to me. She announced to my father as we all sat around on the gold upholstery: "Bob, my purpose for living is over. George was everything. I have no life now."

When the other grown-ups were out of the room, Grandmom told me she had gotten up one night to go to the bathroom and had seen a tall shadow in the hallway. She was going to scream but realized it was just the shadow made from the door standing ajar. She gave her smoker's laugh as she told me this—but it was a nervous sound now. I knew she didn't think it was funny, but I laughed along with her.

I wanted to say, "What do you mean, you don't have a life? Of course you have a life. You're here, and we're here." I was too young to understand the constraints on her.

————————

My mother learned to drive as soon as she got married. She was 20. My father, 27, didn't think women were bad drivers, but he did think for a long time that a woman's domain should be the same as my grandmother's: inside the house, buying groceries, taking us places. And here's something weird: Mom rarely wandered around our yard. She didn't hold anything against outdoor play and even encouraged us to spend a lot of time outside, but she didn't garden, bicycle, or run. She would not play football with us or throw snowballs or rake the leaves.

I liked to run. I liked to stand on one leg, gripping the edge of the kitchen counter and kicking my other leg high, front and back, over and over. I climbed trees. The maple outside our kitchen window had a lovely giant branch that I pretended was the deck of a large ship. I ice-skated with my brothers, circling the rink as fast as we could. Dad taught me how to glide. Mom did not skate with us.

Her rare athletic endeavors were those few mountain climbs we did as a family on vacation.

But she moved fast, all the time. Inside our split-level house, she ran easily up and down four staircases. I watched her chase my brother Steve many times when he refused to do something and got snarky. She would stomp in his direction, glaring at him, and he would dash away from her, up the stairs to his room. Mom could make him hurry.

I also hold this vivid memory: Mom needed to get to the bank before it closed, and she rushed in her high heels across Nassau Street, dodging between moving cars, kicking each foot out at an angle due to the tightness of her skirt.

She always leaned on one hip when she stood, favoring her right leg. Something with her right leg made it hard to run fast. Before I figured it out, I thought she didn't run because her skirts were too narrow. They had no legroom. One could not stride in those skirts. She bought some of those kinds of skirts for me. Even after miniskirts came in, no one could move very freely for all that careful tugging and avoiding bending down.

The real reason she didn't run around much was that, in fact, she had hurt her knee in high school. She played field hockey for a while, though why she quit remains a mystery. She was not tall, but her legs were long for her body, giving her the appearance of height. She moved with a natural grace. One old snapshot captured her darting out of the frame as her boyfriend and mother stood smiling. Even hiding from a camera lens, she looked graceful.

Despite moving fast, Mom forever ran late. As a student at Frankford High School in northeast Philadelphia, she often ran up the down staircase, probably because taking that staircase instead of the correct one would save her twenty seconds. She slipped and fell during one of these dashes, and a sharp pain made her gasp and hold her knee.

Her knee bothered her the rest of her life. Sometimes she seemed to have no problems. She climbed Rattlesnake, Mount Morgan, and Mount Percival, the three New Hampshire mountains our family liked. She moved slowly, true, but she hiked up those boulders and slippery mud patches in white Keds sneakers and orange double-knit bell bottoms with matching sleeveless top and never complained.

———————

One October day during my fourth-grade year, I stepped out of my house dressed in my blue ski pants with stirrups under the feet. The class was taking a field trip to an apple orchard. Our teacher, Mrs. Scibelli, had said that on that day only, girls would be permitted to wear pants. My coat that day was a wool plaid shirttail jacket I usually wore on Saturdays. Something seemed different as I began walking into the chilly sun. What could it be? As I crossed the intersection of Riverside Drive and Prospect Avenue and started up the hill by the maple tree, I realized what it was. *My legs were warm. I could take long strides.*

Probably someone at school teased me about the way my pants looked. But for that moment after leaving the house, I felt truly free in both body and spirit. I had not yet connected that feeling of freedom to climbing mountains. At 9, I thought of mountains as very hard to climb and something to be endured a couple of times a year for the view.

But the person I would become had taken root. I had identified a moment of feeling at home in my body. Later, I would find on mountains an authentic world where I didn't have to seek others' approval for anything. A place where I simply must watch where I walked and get down safely. Where I could speak my mind. In the coming years, I would walk into wild lands where circumstances forced me into surviving on my own strength, if for just a few days. In the world of my childhood, a woman could not find that experience in civilization. So it took me longer than it might have to find it.

———————

Over the past four decades, I have walked up and down thousands of miles in the Northeast mountains with friends, husband, daughters—and alone. My story is that of a woman who felt a little scared of nature growing up— and who learned that nature expanded her sense of independence and self-sufficiency.

My journey over many years has followed a sequence of mountain adventures and realizations of what I could do and how uncomfortable I could be. I have returned again and again to the ridges for wisdom that I take back home. The wild lands have challenged my abilities as a mother, as I pushed my daughters to become independent on awkward, dirty camping trips. I have nurtured a force deep in my heart that I think lies within others who care about these lands. My journey of maturity is rough-hewn, grubby feminism with bouts of fear, anxiety, and desolation; climbs into insight; and moments of elation.

At 23, I knew almost nothing about moving through mountains. I followed others good enough to take me. Five years later I hiked the entire Appalachian Trail with my now-husband Nat and friends Phil and Cay. Several years later, I took my young daughters backpacking on spring vacations. I made many mistakes, which somehow led to getting things right.

In my 40s, I began exploring the White Mountains of New Hampshire and parts of Maine (mostly) with friends and hiking partners. I became editor of the journal *Appalachia*, which connected me even more strongly to the Northeast mountains. By age 49, I resolved to backpack alone, which felt like starting over. The mountains and solitude never lied to me or allowed me to lie. They brought me to my humanity. In some of the deepest loneliness I've ever known, in a wilderness camping spot by myself, I realized that I no longer felt afraid.

My mountain metamorphosis has taken me from naive self-consciousness to purpose and greater spirituality. I do not count myself more than an ordinary pilgrim, and that is more than enough for me. The wild lands have taught me to search for their lonesome winds, which blow through me and which I can never claim.

THE RAMSEY TRAIL

One June weekend not long ago, I stepped onto the Ramsey Trail. This path shoots up the face of West Rattlesnake Mountain, my family's favorite hill in central New Hampshire. I hesitated. The boulder-strewn trail would require more time than I had just then. I hadn't crab-walked up this cliff in so long. Midday sun glittered on the mica bits in the dry soil. Roots hunched up beside the old rocks. The vegetation seemed so familiar, and yet the trees had grown much larger and the path more trampled since I was small.

I'd been climbing mountains for so many years that I was shocked to find myself back in childhood. I imagined I could hear my three brothers' voices. Steve, five years older than me, was saying, "Chrissie, we're not going to wait." John, my closest brother, was scrambling his way up, baggy jeans hanging, calling, "Chrissie, come on." Bob, six years older, was quietly surging forward. (I also remembered a time on the Ramsey when Bob was in his late 20s, a microchip engineer. We were racing my father up the mountain.

Climbs spanning my entire life came together in one powerful, uncomfortable realization as I pushed up the face, looking nervously at my watch because some people were going to be waiting for me down below. I realized that I'd learned to scale mountains through a kind of tough tiger-brother training. None of my brothers ever waited for me. They never asked how I was feeling or if I thought the climb was too hard. When I complained about their bombastic indifference, my parents would say, "They give you a hard time because they like you."

Panting, I lunged toward the steepest part after briefly going the wrong way. I'd gotten lost right here as a teenager, the only other time I'd come this way alone. Some years later, my husband and I followed Bob, who was by then a microchip engineer, on this same wrong fork. He realized the mistake and then sighed, "We've lost seven minutes!"

The friendly competition going up this face had bothered me in childhood. That was it! I'd dreaded mountains when I was a kid, but they always exerted this amazing force, and I kept going up, over and over. Many years later, when I found the mountains again, I knew something. I knew in muscle memory that pain is not a bad thing. When you climb to the top of even a very small mountain, by the hardest route possible, you know that you can do more hard things. This is the epitome of developing resilience.

Steve later told me that he believed nobody could keep up with him and John on the Ramsey Trail. "One particular time," he said, "Dad got the big idea that the men, and you, would all climb up Ramsey together." He recalled that I had caused some kind of commotion because I thought a bee had stung me. "You slowed down, then stopped, and began whining about it. Dad—and I think Bob—stayed behind to attend to you, and John and I finished off the trail alone at our usual pace. Inwardly, I was a little annoyed we had to deal with you—no bee sting was ever verified—but it all worked out in the end." I remember nothing about a bee sting, and I note the happy oddness of Steve's saying that "it all worked out in the end." When I was a kid, running behind them, I was never sure whether it all was working out at all.

John reminded me, when I asked, of the time he and I went up with our father, "the great trail finder" (which he wasn't, being from cities originally, and part of this dynamic was him laughing at himself and our learning to follow trails so *he* wouldn't get lost). "In true form," John said, "we lost the trail about halfway up. Then we just bushwhacked. Somehow, we eventually found our way to the top. I remember you were not too happy about losing the trail, but you soldiered on and got it done."

I remember that particular day well. I trusted them. I guess it was just part of the family business, to scramble up Rattlesnake at every opportunity during our two short weeks.

Now, back after so many years, I instinctively hurried as if still following the boys. All of my brothers were athletes. They did not consider any other method of climbing but going as fast as possible. I could match their pace or I could hang back. My choice. My brothers sometimes intimidated me, but they radiated pure joy on Rattlesnake.

I glanced at the sparkling water of the lake far below. Then I hurried down, crab-walking and jumping from rock to root, shocked at how strong the boys' presence felt. And I soon realized why. For all the times I'd climbed Rattlesnake—by the Col and Ridge trails, by the Pasture Trail, by

The summit of West Rattlesnake Mountain, overlooking Squam Lake, New Hampshire.

the old Bridle Path, and by this crazy Ramsey Trail—this moment marked the first time I had been on the Ramsey by myself. I had tried to walk it alone once, as a teenager, and taken the wrong trail, ending up in a meadow 25 minutes later.

The boys were the reason I climbed mountains, and yet when I got serious about it—that year when my husband, two friends, and I set out to thru-hike the Appalachian Trail—I later learned that only John predicted I would make it. Steve and Bob were not sure. But each of them came out to meet us on the trail. Steve and his wife waited for us at Pine Grove Furnace State Park. John and his wife hiked with us into Palmerton, Pennsylvania. Bob waited at a trailhead in Vermont overnight, packed in two cans of baked beans for us, and hiked with us for half a day.

Not one word of doubt. Instead, my brothers all showed by their actions that they trusted me, just as they had so long ago.

THE BROKEN SANDAL AND THE CLIPBOARD

This essay deals extensively with issues of weight and body dysmorphia, including one mention of pound numbers at age 14. This section begins on page 18 and concludes on page 23.

For many years I settled into a pattern when my family went to New Hampshire. My brothers and my father wanted to climb mountains in the Squam Range or the White Mountains most mornings and sometimes all day. My mother wanted to shop at the craft stores. My little sister, Anne, was still so small that her climbing amounted to riding on Steve's shoulders. I wanted to do everything. So some days I'd go shopping with Mom and Anne, watching Mom pick out lampshades with pressed leaves and flowers and handwoven fabrics. Other days I'd climb with the boys. I went up Mounts Morgan,

John and I climbing Mount Percival. *Christine Woodside archive*

Percival, Moriah, and the Rattlesnakes. Some of them many times.

One morning when I was about 12, I was sitting in the front seat of the station wagon with Mom at the wheel. We were dropping off the boys at the Mount Morgan trailhead; then she, Anne, and I would head down to Center Sandwich to look at the League of New Hampshire Craftsmen store.

On Mount Percival with (from left) Steve, my father, and John. *Christine Woodside archive*

Suddenly, as Dad and my brothers moved away from the car across the dusty pull-off, I said, "I'm going to climb!" Mom nodded. And I jumped out of the car. I was wearing thong sandals.

Near the top, as I pushed my feet against the rocks and steep ground, the leather piece that went between my big and second toe pulled away from the base. The sandal bottom started flapping uselessly. My bare foot gripped the dry dirt. Dad and I were talking about his childhood. Maybe he was telling one of his stories about how he felt left out on the playground. He had switched schools a lot as a kid; he knew what loneliness felt like. I didn't want to slow down the proceedings since the boys were ahead of us. So I just told Dad I was fine and spent the rest of the climb curling my toes in a somewhat useless attempt to keep the leather sole in between me and the ground. Going down was definitely a trick. I don't remember complaining. I just talked with Dad, endlessly, about everything. He would listen to me, and it was effortless to chatter to him.

Forever after, Dad would remind me—whenever I was facing anything physically hard—that I had climbed a 2,220-foot-high mountain in flapping foot gear. Run a mile race in the rain? "You can do that," he'd say. "Remember the time you climbed Mount Morgan with the broken sandal?"

The body grows.

Soon after my broken-sandal triumph, my physical self began to change. I grew breasts. My legs and stomach felt heavier, although I was still a beanpole. It wasn't as easy to skip around. Adolescence was when the body that had leaped, jumped, and kicked joyfully through life gradually transformed into a new vessel I had to learn how to inhabit.

The weird part is that although the process took several years, my recognition of imprisonment inside my changing body hit me suddenly on one Saturday afternoon in early spring. It was something an adult asked me to do.

For seven years, I had loved dancing. I took lessons at the Princeton Ballet Society on Alexander Road, right near the tracks that carried commuters from downtown Princeton to Princeton Junction and on to New York. We'd hear the whistle in the middle of most classes and have to stop for a moment because we couldn't hear the music or teacher while the train screeched by. Pure joy, doing pirouettes and grande battements and piqué turns and coaxing our legs into full splits. I was no more than 5-foot-3 with legs and arms too long for my body.

The school was putting on the ballet *Coppélia*, the story of a dollmaker who falls in love with the life-sized doll he's built. She becomes real, and after charming him, she destroys his workshop as a joke. Actually, a local girl has impersonated the doll and tricked him. The second act ends with him sobbing in his wrecked store.

It's a tragedy, but it includes a lot of happy scenes: a mazurka (a fast three-time Polish dance), "Waltz of the Hours," and lovely moments in the shop. I was cast in two parts. They put me in the mazurka and in a character role playing the wooden Coppélia doll before she seems to come alive. For that, I got to stand up jerkily in the window, lift a book to my eyes, turn right and left, and then sit down, all while the dollmaker blew me kisses. The whole bit took about 40 seconds.

For the mazurka, my brain could not function to remember the moves. We were supposed to circle in two lines very fast and then immediately start executing complicated steps in character shoes, which are leather street-style dancing shoes with straps and stiff soles. I'd never worn character shoes. I had never had to find my way in a dance where everyone moved in different positions. I kept following the wrong people and forgetting what to do. The teachers moved me to "Waltz of the Hours," a lyrical piece with at least a dozen dancers performing traditional ballet steps. That felt more familiar but still beyond my abilities. I had to practice alone with the leader after rehearsal just to get my part down. My mother was on the staff of the ballet school and made costumes. She was always around the studio. I felt embarrassed if I couldn't do something. But I held on, and I did so love to dance.

Then came the clipboard incident.

We were at a rehearsal in the studio running *Coppélia* from start to finish. These run-throughs always lasted hours, and dancers sat around waiting for their parts. I was supposed to be doing homework while not performing, but I couldn't stop watching the lead dancers, who were so, so good. Sitting up front, inspecting everything, with her right leg curled under her and her left leg crossed over, sat Mrs. E., the elegant, ancient (it seemed to me) ballet director. I adored her. She believed the human form to be beautiful, and she inspired us to express beauty with our arms, legs, and whole bodies. Her husband, Mr. E., was there, too. He often helped out with rehearsals, even though his real job was teaching English.

That day, Mrs. E. had told me I could learn the part of the soldier doll by practicing on the side if I didn't get in anyone's way. I joyfully stepped into imaginary sword jabs, and checking my position in the side mirrors while watching the soldier doll with one eye. Then the rehearsal took a break. Mr. E. started walking around the room holding a clipboard, going up to each girl and writing something down.

When he approached me, I stood up and walked to the center of the studio to meet him. He showed me his clipboard, which had a list of all the dancers on the left side of a paper. On the right side, across the top, he had written, "Pounds to lose."

"Christine, see your column here? I've put down 7. You should lose 7 pounds," he said. I noticed that some of the other dancers also had to lose 7 pounds. Some had to lose more, and some less.

"How do I lose 7 pounds?" I asked.

He explained I would do it by eating less. And that I would look very good for dancing afterward. I tried to understand this. I had seen the blobs of cottage cheese in the photo of the Dieter's Protein Plate at the local diner, but I had never thought about what it must be like to go on a diet.

Mrs. E. clapped her hands and started the rehearsal again. I went over to the side mirrors to continue shadowing the soldier doll. But now, as the recorded music swelled and I checked the mirror, I saw a round stomach under my light blue leotard. Too much flesh. A body that was not acceptable. I tried to smile at my reflection as before, but I no longer felt happy. This was the start of a long battle in my mind about my body. Was it a vessel for joyful living, or was it a prison? It became more like a barrier than a tool. A foe, something that didn't look the way I felt or serve me the way I wanted it. A trap.

I was 14 years old. I weighed about 110 pounds.

At home, Mom said she would pack diet lunches for me. She said she knew all about losing weight, and she would tell me what to eat. This was an assignment. A task I must master, like learning math or a piqué turn. I could not yet see into the full-on sorrow and self-criticism my name on the clipboard had released. But I began feeling proud of myself if I felt hungry and deprived or, alternately, feeling ashamed if I ate for any reason, such as celebration or boredom or even to satisfy hunger. Throughout most of my teen years, I would fantasize about curling up in a chair and kind of disappearing and hate the fact that I couldn't do that.

My body dysmorphia did not lead to the better-known forms of eating disorders. It eventually took the forms of rebellion and anger. Rebellion: I insisted on eating if I felt hungry. I would not deprive myself. Oh, I would try to diet for a few weeks. Then I would give up and, hours after dinner, return to the kitchen and eat leftovers out of the pot of spaghetti or whatever was still sitting at the back of the stove; sometimes my mother would come in and say, "Uh-uh-uh. . . . " I would skitter out of the kitchen and upstairs.

It was a ridiculous exercise, dieting when I didn't need to diet and trying to change my body to meet arbitrary standards. I was learning how to be very angry but to keep that feeling deep inside, to suppress my anger at people I loved and respected telling me I was not good enough unless I could stunt my own natural growth. I moved anger around, I suppose. I'm not trying to become a psychologist when I'm not one. But I do know that I felt despair that even if I made the goal of losing 7 pounds, I would never feel free again. If I played it their way, I would never be able to eat just because I felt hungry. I was learning that I could not trust the most basic instinct of being alive, which is eating when one needs fuel. It was so very twisted, this culture my ballet school created. I think they hoped it would make us stronger. Instead I felt deficient.

I honestly don't recall if I was able to lose 7 pounds or not. The school didn't hold weigh-ins. I carried little diet lunches to eighth grade all that spring. By fall, I had decided, with my brother John's urging, to go out for the cross-country team, so I started running every day, and the question of dieting was moot. We were in great shape; we burned off a lot of calories and ate full meals, with snacks, and my mom did not control my food in any way for a while. That June I finished seventh in New Jersey's state final of the girls' mile run.

But after my first year of running competitively, I overtrained and had what must have been a stress injury or plantar fasciitis. I couldn't run without a lot of pain and had to drop out of the cross-country season. I only ran for a portion of winter track, and by spring, I couldn't run a quarter-mile without extreme pain. So I quit the team. And I began to gain a little weight, the way any developing woman gains weight. Months later, after I could finally run again, I didn't know how to run with a woman's body.

Then the dieting game began again. I hated dancing because that world had created that game. Yet I had stepped into the strange new wilderness of their beauty standard. I hated myself that year I turned 16. A boy I fell in love with dropped me for someone else. I descended into a depression that was so bad I didn't like anything in my life. I felt ugly. I'd make plans and proclamations in my diary about "losing the weight, dammit," believing that if I were as thin as I had been at age 14, I'd be content. And yet I understood that I could not live happily in constant deprivation.

I'd lose a few pounds and then get tired of hunger. I'd decide to eat if I wanted to, and I would gain weight back. I never ate great amounts or purged; I was too squeamish, perhaps, to become bulimic, but I did go through periods where I ate more than I truly wanted and gained a few pounds. Then I'd hate myself for lack of discipline, for failing to look the way I imagined I should, for missing my potential. I would briefly try dieting again and lose a few pounds but then feel so hungry that the cycle would start over. Now, when I look at photos of myself from those years, I see I was never overweight, not even during times I believed I was fat.

My sister, Anne, became a professional dancer some years later, and her stage career helped me resurrect my love of dance. Anne had a healthy attitude about dance and her body. She seemed to take it in stride when her directors told dancers to lose a few pounds. She loved dance as much as I loved the mountains.

Three months after I returned from hiking the Appalachian Trail, I went to see Anne perform the role of Snow Queen in "The Nutcracker" at the Trenton War Memorial theater. I had never seen her dance with a partner before. The man lifted her above his shoulders and she rotated around in the air like a fairy. Her long legs and arms seemed to reach naturally out of her beautiful back as the fake snowflakes sifted down. I cried. This was what dance was supposed to be. She was magnificent. After the first act ended and the curtain dropped onto the leftover snowflakes, I made my way to the stage door and intercepted her backstage. I cried out and we started hugging. Her costume's scratchy decorations brushed my hand as I reached to tighten my grip.

Anne said, "Are you crying?"

I said, "Yes. Are you crying?" We both nodded. I was still recovering from my long hike; my knees were a little sore, but my body finally felt like my own. And now I could appreciate dance from the outside. Release my anger about dance, and feel happy for a true dancer.

I will always be grateful that watching her dance rehabilitated my fury into loving the purity of dance, the joy of movement, which is not different from the joy I feel dancing across boulders.

What I really wanted was to feel as free in my body as I had felt all through childhood. Running and leaping without worrying how I looked. Never thinking about scales or comparing myself to models. I had finally discovered the place where I could feel comfortable in my body and mind. Where the two could come together, beautifully. Where I could be at ease in my mind, accepting and valuing my physical strength. That place was the mountains.

THE BATTERED POT

Sometime in the late 1970s, my old friend Peter told me, he was sitting in a ridge-top campsite in Montana, popping popcorn in his little aluminum pot on a camp stove. Something went wrong. The pot fell off the stove and started rolling down the mountain. Peter crashed through the trees after it. He searched and searched for the blackened 2-pint pot hiding in the brush and finally grabbed it and took it back up to his campsite.

He told this story as he was popping popcorn in that same pot in August 1983. He had taken me and three others backpacking. We had just finished our 2-month jobs as camp counselors at Pioneer Village in Deep River, Connecticut. The day the kids all got on the bus or climbed into their parents' cars, Peter was poring over a small orange-covered 1972 *White Mountain Guide* while sitting on the collapsing couch in the staff building. I overheard him talking to my boyfriend, Nat, and my friend Phil. They pointed at maps. I did not go over to look. I knew he was eager to take us out for four days and three nights. We would be sleeping in tents. I didn't really understand the route until I set my borrowed suede Bass boots onto the trail near New Hampshire's Crawford Notch, but I can say now that we were outfitting ourselves to hike over Mount Zealand and the Twin Range, across Garfield Ridge, and over to Mount Lafayette.

I was 24 now. I had never hiked any of those mountains and had only the vaguest idea of where they were. The one White Mountain peak I'd climbed was Mount Moriah with my dad and a group from Rockywold-Deephaven Camps, when I was 14.

Nat put gear into an old backpack he'd borrowed for me. He said I should use a down sleeping bag, not the rectangular-ended camp bag I'd used inside the platform tent all summer. He gave me a nylon stuff sack and told me to pack my raincoat and some warm clothes, plus extra socks. Back then, we all took woven cotton. I packed jeans, a T-shirt, and a flannel shirt. I shoved extra ragg wool socks, T-shirts, and underwear into the stuff stack.

Kit (left), Peter, and I (in the borrowed hat) getting breakfast at Guyot Campsite. *Nat Eddy*

Our friend Kit, who'd also worked at camp that summer, told me it was a good idea to take a wool hat and lent me one.

The sun was low in the sky at about 6 P.M. when we stepped onto the Ethan Pond Trail. (I didn't know the name of the trail then. I just knew I was following Peter, Phil, Nat, and Kit.) The path was bare dirt, the slant uphill reminding me of the Squam Range mountains I had climbed with my family. Up, up, up. The trail took a few hairpin switchbacks. Phil turned around and said, "Whoa." This was steep. These loads were so heavy. I don't remember thinking or feeling much, just following. When they moved forward, I did. When they stopped, I did. I was very strong, but I did not know this.

An hour or so up, the trees thinned out, and we stepped across a big boulder at the edge of a little lake. It was nearly dark now, and we trudged up to the edge of a shelter, where several hikers sat on the edge of the open front. One of them pointed us to a sloping area set among spruce trees. It was now getting so dark that I just followed Nat and did what he said, crawling into the small tent he set up. The chill descended. Dead quiet.

The next thing I remember was sitting half up inside my sleeping bag. I could hear noises outside the tent door. Roaring noises, almost like small jets. A few muffled voices broke through the jet-engine sounds. I poked my head out. From where I sat, I could see four or five hikers sitting or squatting, tending small pots on top of tiny camp stoves. The stoves were making the noise. Close to our tent sat a woman in a wool cap and a heavy jacket. Her stove, too, roared.

Wrinkles lined her forehead and framed her eyes; she was not young. She stirred something in a pot on her jet-engine stove. She stared into the morning without smiling and without acknowledging me. Then she looked down at her bubbling breakfast and stirred it with a small spoon. She was alone, not in tow as I was. She adjusted something on the stove's side. Behind her I could see the glittering water of Ethan Pond. I wonder now if my jaw was hanging open, watching her among all of those experienced hikers, many of them solo hikers, getting themselves up and ready. The woman obviously had done all this many times before. She was comfortable. And I sensed that for her, being comfortable here did not involve relaxing, laughing, or goofing around. She looked like a woman who understood herself, knew and respected her surroundings, and could work with her particular strengths and her limitations. I knew right then that I wanted to be like her. I wanted to feel that way out here, because right then, I did not.

The sun rose a bit, shedding a little warmth onto the site. Someone said, "Let's go skinny-dipping!" The five of us walked down to the edge of the water. I had my Minolta SRT-101 with me; my first instinct was to take pictures. I caught the bare buns of my friends as they entered the pond. Then I stripped out of my long johns and flannel shirt and stepped into the frigid water. I had done this many times in Squam Lake, south of here, in the end-of-summer chill, and so I did as I had always done: waded out to waist-deep water and dove under as fast as I could. Then I sighed with joy and retreated, stepping fast over slippery underwater rocks back to the shore. I tried to flick last year's spruce needles from my feet, but they stuck on, leaving a lovely piney sap smell. I struggled into my clothes and followed the others back to our tents. The woman was gone. I never knew where she was headed, and I never saw her again. But I would never stop thinking about her.

A few hours later, as I trudged behind Peter, Nat, Phil, and Kit, the trail turned onto an old railroad bed that had once been used to carry logs out of the area. The imposing Whitewall Mountain rose above us as we came to an intersection that led Peter to stop and pull out a map. "We could take the Zeacliff Trail," he said, but I couldn't make out the rest. Since childhood, I had struggled with hearing loss, mostly in my right ear. But at the time, I still didn't realize that was the cause for missing conversations in outdoor settings like this. I thought they were excluding me from a decision. Which way would we go?

I heard Kit: "No. I'd like to see Zealand Hut and walk around on the old railroad bed. I'll go that way and meet up with you later." Nat and Phil were saying something about taking the trail that tumbled steeply down to our left. I didn't know which trail would be a better route for my sensibilities, but a surge of competitive energy boiled up in me. I sensed that if I took the trail on the old railroad bed, I would not be challenging myself—or something. I didn't know what I wanted to do. I only knew that I felt left out of the map discussion, so I didn't understand what was at stake. Peter decided he'd hike with Kit, and they set off. "Why didn't you show me the map?" I fumed at Nat. He and Phil gestured that they would step onto the rough trail, the Zeacliff.

"Which way should I go?" I asked. They did not answer. They had decided the way they would go, and Kit and Phil had chosen their route, but I was not even sure where we *were* relative to the other landmarks on the map. So I didn't understand the choices. I had peered at the map with them, and although I had no idea then that many contour lines close together mean a very steep scramble, I still could not get clear where we were standing and where we were headed. I had too much to learn.

I sighed angrily. There they went, and I was not going to be left behind.

"F— you!" I yelled at my boyfriend. He and Phil looked startled at my anger and began hiking fast; I was right on their heels. The trail was hellish. It bumbled down on boulders and soon began to climb steeply up an impossible rocky slope. Why had I come this way? I knew something was wrong with my attitude, but I could not begin to fix it. I felt ridiculous that I had left so much to the others. I was truly in tow here. I had simply been following the group, and I was following Nat and Phil now, and I was pissed. At them. At myself.

Fury can help with getting up a cliff. We emerged just south of Zeacliff itself. I didn't know why this way was any better. But I had kept up with Nat and Phil. We rested a while, waiting for Kit and Peter to catch up. Kit said the hut had been great, and Peter agreed. I envied the others' calm certainty about which route was best for them. They didn't have anything to prove, whereas I thought I had everything to prove.

We regrouped, I stopped feeling mad—maybe I was too tired—and Peter led us along the Twinway. Soon we emerged out of the trees onto Mount Guyot. Its rocky expanse swept away from us toward South Twin. We turned left and soon arrived at our campsite. The sun began to go down, and I put on my wool hat and watched the others pull out the two stoves and cook dinner. Nat set up our tent.

Nat had brought a cute metal clamshell Optimus kit that opened up into a little white-gas stove. Morning and evening, he filled it with gas, pumped a primer knob, and fussed with it until it roared to life. The rectangular pot was part of the kit lid. Water boiled like a roiling sea. He poured in a red powder and commanded, "Dissolve, you wormlike tomato substance."

The next morning, we climbed the slight rise out of the campsite back to the ridge just below Guyot. We hiked along a kind of undulating ocean of rock dotted with rock cairns from North Twin Mountain to South Twin, peering across what felt like a thousand years. This section of the Twinway grabbed hold of me, like a view of my own future, and I transitioned out of the world of self-consciousness and into one where I began speaking to myself from the inside. Peter was a veteran hiker from the West, and I began to notice his ease with his gear and his slow, steady pace. He introduced all

Not happy, probably at the end of the Zeacliff Trail. *Nat Eddy*

of us to the magic world of getting up onto a ridge and, basically, not coming down until we had forgotten where we used to live.

A few months later, Peter gave me and Nat the old pot. I still use it. It's been to the Rockies, up Bigelow Mountain in Maine (twice), along the entire 2,100 or so miles of the Appalachian Trail, on the Long Trail in Vermont, and through parts of the White Mountain National Forest dozens of times. It's served meals in Tennessee, North Carolina, Virginia, and near home in Connecticut. That pot must have broken some kind of record.

I hang on to it because I like its compact shape, but mostly because it almost fell off a mountain and was rescued by Peter, whom I haven't seen in decades. It embodies so many years of experience.

My love for that pot borders on the irrational. An ancient Coleman Peak One backpacking stove fits neatly inside it. The pot lid has a convenient little knob that doesn't burn my fingers, even though the lid is so misshapen now that it alternately falls off or gets stuck.

The pot undulates because of many dents on the bottom. "That pot is listing!" a hiker friend scolded once, shaking his head as my morning water boiled. I demonstrated the pot one June morning in Connecticut before a stunned crop of long-distance hikers. They seemed amazed that this setup still worked after the same number of years they'd been alive. The younger hikers were boiling one cup at a time on little alcohol stoves that weighed nothing. I wondered if I'd become an inflexible kook.

Yes, probably. My pot connects me to the 1970s, when Peter got it. The pot says so much. It says I have done this long enough that I know what I am doing. It says that I like living and cooking slowly in the woods rather than moving through at breakneck speed. It says I will not compromise my habits and comfort to save a few ounces. It says that old, simple things can mean more than new, perfect ones.

When I stir bubbling soup in the battered pot, I am not only in the mountains but somewhere else: on the Twinway in 1983, following Peter and the others from cairn to cairn. In my imagination, I stop and pull out my Minolta camera, framing rocks, hikers, and composure.

EIGHT LEGS

I lay on my back on a flimsy sleeping pad on a dirty wooden floor in an open-fronted shelter. Nat and our friends Phil and Cay lay next to me. Phil held a thin paperback book high above his head, the cover bent back beneath his grasping hand. He tipped the page toward the beam of his tiny flashlight. I stared up at the outlines of endless leaves. The dusk sank in. Phil's smooth voice lulled the three of us. He was reading from "Burnt Norton," the first part of T. S. Eliot's work *Four Quartets*. "Time present and time past / Are both perhaps present in time future."

Four days earlier, we had started walking the Appalachian Trail through the tree-covered mountains of northwest Georgia. We were four of the hundreds of ordinary Americans-turned-pilgrims, redeeming the regrets of bad jobs, unrealized ambitions, and goals we felt dimly might exist if we could identify them. We would push ourselves through this adventure, and (I predicted) it would change us. We would live in the present and walk with heavy packs for as long as we could—we planned on covering all 2,096 miles (the length of the AT at that time), through the ridges of Tennessee and North Carolina, Virginia, West Virginia, Maryland, Pennsylvania, New Jersey, New York, Connecticut, Massachusetts, Vermont, New Hampshire, and Maine. We had quit our jobs and vacated our apartments. We thought that what we were doing made sense.

The Journey Taken

Phil read from the book about memories of journeys never taken and "the door we never opened." My shoulder blades ached. I smelled. The soles of my feet felt smashed and bruised. And on this mid-April night early in our journey, I strained to understand T. S. Eliot. In a few weeks, we would hardly have time to glance at the cover of the *Four Quartets* paperback. But its somber truths matched my state of mind on this new, painful march.

Nat and I had been married for almost two years, Phil and Cay for about ten months. Although we lived a few hundred miles from one another, our connections rooted deeply. Phil and Nat first met at Haverford College and then spent many summers as counselors at Incarnation Camp in Connecticut. Friends introduced me to Nat when he was at Yale Divinity School and I was working as a journalist in Philadelphia. I then joined Nat and Phil at camp. Phil and Nat later worked for Cay at Nature's Classroom, an outdoor education program in New Hampshire.

For two years before we stepped onto the trail, I managed a newspaper in Westchester County, New York. I worked at least 55 hours a week. It felt like a sweatshop. I dedicated myself selflessly to a perfect product, and I was miserable. The more miserable I felt, the harder I worked, thinking this would stop the feeling. It did not. No one ever seemed happy there, no matter how hard we all worked. I began to daydream about, and then plan, a long escape.

The summer when Nat, Phil, and I were counselors together, I found on the staff lounge shelf two giant hardcover books: *Hiking the Appalachian Trail*, volumes 1 and 2 (Rodale Press, 1975). They comprised long narratives by private citizens who had left society and hiked the entire Appalachian Trail, usually in one season but sometimes over multiple years, before the days of social media. The books encased a world of personal agency. Each of the people who thru-hiked in those years lived off the grid. No one would know where exactly they were at any moment unless they told someone. They wanted it that way. I began to wonder if Nat and I could escape in this way for a while. One night, sitting in the bedroom of our apartment in Tarrytown, I broached the idea. Nat jumped up from the bed's edge, where he was taking off his shoes after walking home from work, and ran downstairs to our half-basement living room. I followed him. He picked up the wall phone and dialed. "Who are you calling?" I asked.

"Phil?" he said. It was Phil and Cay in Boston.

They said yes.

Nat sold his shares in the infrared optics business he had helped his old friend Frank establish. Frank was the expert technician, the inspiration, and the brains of the company. Nat was the office manager who hated being office manager and who made himself learn the precise work of polishing tiny windows for heat detectors and other equipment. I barely understood what he was making all day, but at night he came home smelling of pitch, cast iron, and toluene. I knew he and Frank were clashing over business decisions, and sometimes after work Nat lay down on the bed and covered his eyes with his forearm. It was easy to see that he was thinking of making a change.

Phil was employed by a university library. He had taught math at a school but didn't enjoy it. Cay had worked in nature education before going to a university business office where it seemed people spent a lot of time arguing.

All four of us: in transition. Making the decision to leave our jobs turned out to be surprisingly easy. Yet no one we knew thought it made sense to hike nearly 2,100 miles. Quitting work and striking out on a long, grueling slog through the backcountry of the East seemed reckless at best. Fortunately, all of us had parents who kept most of their worries to themselves. They understood that our adventures were our business. When Nat and I stopped over at my in-laws, who lived a few blocks away, I could sometimes feel their amazement. I once walked into their kitchen wearing new hiking boots with my jeans. I'd never owned such boots growing up. I said to my mother-in-law, Tibbie, "When I wear these boots, I feel just wonderful!" She replied, "Well, I think you should keep wearing them, then."

I went out to the trail for more than the obvious reason of disliking my job. Something lay deep within me, unfinished. I sensed that the reason my job was such a burden was the way I approached it. I was like a good soldier, following the rules in a world where I easily could have helped make those rules. My default seemed to be giving strangers and acquaintances a lot of leeway without expecting breathing room for myself. Overwork squeezed out time I could have been running, or walking, or just reading, or hanging out with Nat. I was all out of balance. On the trail, I wanted to try an immensely difficult physical challenge that society did not expect of me. I wanted to grow up emotionally, to step into the more confident, joyful person I knew I could be.

Yet the extreme scale of the path toward maturity became clear quickly. Planning and executing a trip like this felt like a strange dream from which I would not wake up until I realized I had condemned myself and my companions to jail because I thought that jail would deepen me.

The beauty of mountains of northwest Georgia made me gasp. But soon enough I was working so hard that I could not always pay attention to the blue-edged ridges tumbling out before me. At a rocky overlook, we sat down and meditated on how we must get up again in a moment and keep going. Phil and Nat had signed up for graduate school, so we would have to reach Maine by early September. We started in mid-April. We needed to average 15 miles a day for four and a half months.

We laughed a lot, but people laugh in jail. Phil one day performed an imitation of an old comedy routine in which Count Dracula says "Bleah" in a Romanian accent. Every time he said, "Bleah," I laughed like a hyena. Phil and I sang television theme songs from the 1960s. I had not known that I

Nat (leading the line), Cay, and Phil on the Appalachian Trail in Georgia, mid-April 1987.

could sing all the verses of *Green Acres*. The freedom to act completely silly felt good. I hadn't laughed this hard in years. Although I didn't yet appreciate the mountains the way I imagined I was supposed to, I did feel something evolving. I could walk many miles a day, every day, even in those early weeks as we built up to 10 miles, then 12 miles, then 20 miles. I could cover those miles and still laugh genuinely just because I needed to laugh. I began to forget that earnest managing editor I had been before.

––––––––––

Phil read "Burnt Norton" in a clear, perfectly paced, unsentimental voice that suggested he had thought about why we had come to be lying on the ground and why we would be doing so for many months. Our pasts and our futures came together in the moment as we lay in our sleeping bags. We would live with what Eliot called "neither plenitude nor vacancy"— neither too much nor too little of anything. Just enough to get by. Just enough food, just enough money, just enough courage. Distractions would almost break us, again and again—whether in the form of stinging wasps, soaking rain, high winds, or brusque postal clerks.

Only Walk

"East Coker," the second poem in *Four Quartets*, refers to the village where T. S. Eliot's ancestors lived in England before leaving for America, and where Eliot was buried. According to Eliot, in beginnings we find where we will end up. And "For us, there is only the trying. The rest is not our business." This reminded me of Nat, who never flinched from pushing us along, adding miles, keeping us on schedule.

Nat could have walked the distance alone. He could push aside doubts and just go. He made his decisions; as Eliot would say, the rest was not his business. He thought only of the plan and could operate as if with blinders on. We all felt pain, cold, and exhaustion, and Nat accepted this as the bargain he had made. I clung to his stoicism even as I butted against it.

(Months in, as we passed through some of the most difficult terrain in New Hampshire, the rest of us—first I, then Cay, then Phil—would nearly melt down. Nat's commitment never wavered. In the town of Hanover, I said I was going to get off the trail for a few weeks. On Mount Washington several days later, Cay called her parents from a pay phone. Afterward, she was dabbing tears as she blew her nose from an awful head cold; the backdrop of the Great Gulf and miles of distant peaks and clouds could not cheer her up. Days later, Phil contemplated getting on a bus on Route 2 in Gorham and heading home to Boston. None of us left the trail, and I believe that's because Nat never considered it.)

Nat said many times after our thru-hike that the beauty of it was that he had no distractions. We needed simply to get up each day and keep going. He often would say, "I only have one thing I have to do today: walk."

––––––––

On a dark June afternoon, we hiked through northern Virginia and toward the low country of Harpers Ferry, West Virginia, headquarters of the Appalachian Trail Conference. A crisis was brewing. Cay said she hoped we could stop early enough to set up camp properly. She meant, Nat and I realized, that she wanted to surprise Phil for his birthday. We remembered she'd been hoarding a box of instant cheesecake in one of the food bags. At about 5 P.M., the four of us convened on the trail, wondering how much farther to go. Nat wanted to walk three more miles to the next shelter. Cay stood quietly, looking down. Of course, she would not say out loud her birthday surprise. Just then, the forest darkened, as if someone had blotted out the light with a cloth. It was going to rain, hard, and probably thunder and lightning too. Nat stood with his hands on his hips and insisted, "If we keep stopping early all the time, we're never going to make it to Katahdin."

He said this periodically, near the end of a day, and he was right in a grand sense of the journey, but because tiredness felt like a mental state to me, I gave in to them in such moments. It was not that I couldn't grasp we were headed toward Katahdin. I knew intellectually that many small steps day after day would get us there. But trudging through those late afternoons of our homeless pilgrimage, I became an emotional being. However, Nat's tough love worked. I usually got angry and then hiked faster.

But now I directed my attention to Cay, hoping that somehow her cheesecake could happen even while we got our miles in. She said, softly and respectfully, in a quavering voice, "I'm concerned that we should set up camp before it rains." When Cay was upset, she became ultrapolite. None of us said anything. We all knew what we had to do. We'd been through this before. No response meant we would keep going. Cay turned and walked forward. She held her back firm, stoically. We kept walking.

No more than 30 seconds later, the trail in front of us turned even darker than it had been a minute before, if that was possible. Fireflies started blinking as if it were sunset. Now rain pelted down.

The wind whipped up. This was a downpour. The four of us, saying nothing, stopped immediately, took off our packs, and mechanically started setting up camp in the middle of the trail. The raindrops plopped around like giant gumballs. Nat and I shook out our tent and slipped its single curved pole through the fabric sleeves. We would sleep smack in the middle of the hiking superhighway, and it seemed a lovely place to stop.

BOOM. The thunderstorm landed. We jammed in the tent stakes, and the fabric of our tents shivered up into place. I dove into our tent while Nat adjusted the fly. He threw me my damp pack, and I sat against it, hugging my knees. A puddle of water settled around my behind. I could hear mad rustling of fabric in the other tent. Cay was pulling out the dinner bag, sobbing.

We sat in our tents, silent, for many minutes. The rain lightened. Cay called out, "I'm making some dinner." In the shelter of her tent fly, she lit the stove, plopped the pot of water on top, and poured in soup mix. A few minutes later, her hand parted our tent door, handing us soup. Then I heard her spoon hitting the side of the pie pan. She was mixing the birthday cheesecake. Several minutes later, the pan, with half of the dessert left, slid into our tent. I dipped my spoon into the smooth filling and licked it off.

Nat had not succeeded in keeping us to our schedule. We had stopped because of the storm. In sunshine, we would have kept going, I knew. And I think Cay knew. We would push to the limit every day. Storms meant we could stop early. Birthdays did not. But since this was also a birthday, maybe this counted as a party.

Iron Mountain

Eliot's third poem in *Four Quartets*, "The Dry Salvages," is named for rocks off Cape Ann, Massachusetts, which he remembered from his childhood. Whether the waves or weather conceal these rocks or not, they remain the same. A rock, timeless in moving time, reminded me of Cay, who had a Florence Nightingale quality about her: she put the comfort of others foremost in her priorities. Night after night, I slumped on the edge of some filthy shelter platform, watching Cay stand in her boots and pour noodles into the unsteady pot. She stirred, dumped cheese sauce, shook salt and pepper, sprinkled a few dried herbs. She dished dinner into our cheap plastic bowls. Cay made dinner most evenings. She had told me when we all got together the previous winter to order food that had variety and that good-tasting food mattered. She could mix and match dried vegetable soup mix, dried cheese, rice, pasta, lentils, potatoes, and spice mix and make it taste good.

I first bonded with Cay as my calm beacon on an awful, cloudy May 21 at dusk. We didn't know each other well when we started out. I was the only one who hadn't worked with her. So there we were, day 36 of our thru-hike. Our group had been walking for ten hours, through a rainstorm, and gotten behind our itinerary, but we were determined to make 21 miles that day. In one week, my old boss, Myron, was meeting us in Pearisburg and taking us to our car so we could drive to my brother's wedding.

After 6 P.M. we marched across Virginia Route 603 and a few minutes later emerged at a driveway near a stream. According to the guidebook, Hurricane Campground lay about 7 miles farther. Nat and Phil thought they could make faster time than all four of us could trying to stay together. We agreed they would go ahead and set up camp before dark. Cay and I would follow as fast as we could.

As they raced off, Cay and I knew that we'd be hiking in the dark.

Don't talk, I thought. The air faded grayer and grayer. I dragged myself into a lumbering gallop behind Cay's fast trot. Cay obviously had calculated that she and I ought to make about 4 miles an hour if we wanted to get there by sunset, which would be at about 8:15. I only knew that I must follow her. I wanted to avoid getting weepy tonight.

The trail twisted one way and then another on a low ridge, Iron Mountain. It meandered up and around hillocks. Cay paused periodically to look back and check for me. As soon as she'd see me catching up, she'd take off again. The sun was making its final dip behind the trees. Cay reached for the guidebook; 2 miles more, up one final treed mountain. I nodded miserably. This would be the evening's last real climb. She stopped, took off her pack, and pulled out the gallon Ziploc bag of raisins. Squatting, we grabbed handfuls and munched as fast as we could. I left my pack on, of course.

Cay could see I was barely holding on. She knew better than to engage me in talk. I just silently hated everything. We stood up. Cay put on her pack.

Then she gently nudged me into the lead. She knew I was strong going uphill. She knew I had a way of igniting out of my doldrums at odd times. So I put my feet one after the other on the incline. Brown leaves and rocks faded as the sky darkened. I kept thinking, *I can still see. I can still see.* The light dissipated into blotches. We knew that if we used our flashlights, our night vision would bleach out, so we kept on in the darkness. The only noises were our boots dully slapping against the dirt and our panting.

Near the crest, I stopped and turned around. "Is this still the trail?" Cay stepped ahead, pulled off her pack, and got out her flashlight, but before we could focus on the beam, we heard voices—strange men's voices, Nat's and Phil's voices, and a dog barking. The animal bounded up to us. I was afraid of dogs, but Cay reached her hand down and let the beast sniff. I wasn't afraid of the dog with her there. Suddenly I felt really good.

Great Dismal Swamp

The final chapter in *Four Quartets* examines suffering as the way to new life. The poem "Little Gidding" is named for an English village where members of an Anglican commune lived in the 1600s, but the group scattered during the mid-century English Civil War. This poem made me think of myself. Hiking the trail had been my idea, and I was the weakest of the four. I cried when I was hungry. I cried when I was tired. I felt that complaining was the way to happiness. And, out of respect, everyone ignored me.

We were hiking through central Virginia near the Great Dismal Swamp. The rain and fog had started around lunchtime, and the rain poured for about three hours. The trail followed roads here, so everything was asphalt, and fast cars swished puddles, sending giant waves onto us. We wobbled along a narrow concrete edging of a one-lane bridge under construction. I felt like my feet were decomposing. A thick layer of calluses absorbed so much water that they were rubbery. Underneath the calluses, giant blisters formed, one on the ball of each foot. It hurt so much to walk that I cried out with each step. By late afternoon, at Nat's suggestion, I switched from my sodden leather boots to the light Adidas running shoes I usually wore in camp at night. I was no less soaked, but I could feel a tiny bit more of my dead feet.

A pathway of bog bridges—two split logs resting flat side up—lay across the wet terrain through here. I stepped onto the wet wood; tingly pain blasted from my feet up into my legs. I screamed. Nat looked back at me with slight disgust. The rain was slowing down now, becoming a misty, chilly cloud.

The clearing for the Wapiti I shelter barely went beyond the buildings and the mushy-looking fire pit in front of it. The inside wasn't too horribly wet. I eased myself to the edge, groaning as I sat down and pulled off those running shoes.

"Chris, why don't you cook dinner?" Nat asked.

I never cooked dinner. Well, I'd done it twice. Usually, Cay in her quiet way started cooking when we reached camp, but that night, they all wanted me to do it. On some level, they understood that I needed rehabilitation.

I roused myself and stopped blubbering. I rummaged through my pack for the first-aid kit and pulled the needle and matches from the red nylon pouch. Somehow, I had to pop those gigantic blisters. I perched on the damp platform with one foot on my other knee, jabbed the needle through the dead white flesh, felt nothing. The pus seeped out, and I wiped it with my bandanna and unwrapped a bandage. Nat handed me my hiking boots; they were sort of dry, while the Adidas now were soaked. I pushed my numb feet back into the boots and left the laces dangling. I stood up, leaning at the edge of the shelter floor. Tomorrow we were going into Pearisburg, Virginia, so we could eat anything out of the packs now; there would be a good opportunity to replenish the stocks. Now it was my job to creatively use up what we had left. I took a seconds-long inventory and then began cooking the last of the dried sliced potatoes. When they softened in the liquid, I dumped mashed-potato flakes into them. Next, I boiled some rice and mixed in more water and leek and potato soup mix as a sauce.

My feet screamed as I stood mixing and stirring the potato-heavy meal, but something gentled my complaints. I had to pay attention to that stove. I started to joke around, pretending I was an Italian chef and saying, "*Mangia, mangia.*" Then I'd giggle hysterically. By the time I handed the glop to my companions, the responsibility of feeding them had quieted my breathing.

Eliot wrote that one must "put off / sense and motion" in a journey. One is not there to prove anything but rather "to kneel / Where prayer has been valid."

I was stumbling in prayer. I remembered the afternoon a few weeks earlier when I realized that I had chosen a life of walking through a tunnel of green and brown leaves. That's really what hiking the Appalachian Trail is. Oh yes, there are open ridges, but mostly you're in the leaves on the way up and on the way down. On that day, we had gotten over a ridge of grassy-topped mountains on the Tennessee–North Carolina border and in mid-afternoon we'd crossed North Carolina Route 226 at Iron Mountain Gap.

The asphalt held onto the sun to mock us. I wanted to scream as I focused on the painted lines pointing to civilization miles away, out of reach. I climbed the rock steps leading from the road back into the woods. The swath of leaves stretched away into the forest. Someone said we had only 6 miles to go. Only 6 miles. I gulped. My chest lurched. The leaves blurred, and I was sobbing. I was walking on ruined feet on endless runners of dead leaves. Nothing would change. It would never feel better, but I was still too proud to give up, so I was going to have to hate every second. There was no talking to me. I waved off every advance from Nat and Phil and Cay. The leaves and tree trunks canopied a horrible highway down which I must march without seeing past it. Crying had once cleansed me. Now I kept crying and only felt worse. I had given up my job and my life and dragged my husband and our friends onto this trail. And I didn't want to do it anymore. I hated every step. I hated my pack. I hated the guidebook, the cheery hiker registers with jaunty remarks like *Goin' all the way!!!* I hated the slimy pepperoni on crumbling crackers. I hated the stale instant coffee. The only thing I wanted was to get out of there. But no. I didn't want to give up. And yet I might have to. Pains shot through my feet and toes. My knees ached constantly. My shoulder blades stung where the pack straps rubbed. I felt exhausted. All the time.

I sat on the edge of the Clyde Smith Shelter that evening, unlacing my boots without even seeing them, tears draining. A man about my age, out with his father, asked me, "I'm interested to know—is it hard to enjoy the trail when you are trying to hike the whole thing?" He said he was on a short trip and soon would start a job as caretaker of a shelter site on Bigelow Mountain in Maine.

I don't know why I held back—perhaps because if I cried out that I was miserable, he might not want to start that job. I simply said, "This is not the best time to ask me that. I've had a bad day today." He nodded kindly, as if taking stock of the population he'd be tending soon. I sat. Cay made dinner. Phil ran water through the hand pump for tomorrow's supply. Nat got out the sleeping bags.

"And what you thought you came for / is only a shell, a husk of meaning," Eliot wrote. The reason I came, in Eliot's take, could not be revealed that evening but over time and motion, as I saw this through. Movement would bring out the meaning, which I could not know yet.

I did know that day, though, that I could not do anything alone. I could not do anything without a strong inner sense of purpose, either.

Sometimes I asked myself if what ailed my generation was that we had not had to go to war. Were we soft? Walking the AT provided a stateside boot camp for my life. I wanted to be strong in case any emergency came: natural disasters, acts of war, accidents.

The days, weeks, and months compressed into a string of repeated rituals that started with the early morning sound of Phil dipping the dishes in boiling water and Nat stirring cereal glop in the giant aluminum pot. By 7 A.M. we were snaking up the path, arms crossed in front of us, gigantic packs swaying behind. "You should see these guys," our friend Jim told someone. "They're an eight-legged thing." And so, months into the journey, we had our trail name, the Eight-Legged Thing. In "thing" formation, Cay led, Phil and I went in the middle because both of us had bad hearing, and Nat was last, pushing us on with his invisible cattle prod.

A typical day went like this: 5 miles, then a snack of six Duplex Creme cookies; 5 miles, then crumbling crackers with peanut butter for lunch; 5 miles, more Duplex Cremes; 5 miles, stop for the night. Cay made dinner while the men pumped water through our filter for the next day; we ate; I washed the dishes wearing my flashlight on its cord around my forehead. Late at night, I awoke, wrote a few sentences in my notebook, and planned our itineraries for the coming days. Each day, we again covered more ground than we felt capable of. Daily hardships pulled me through by their rituals. In new rituals, I broke away from my former life of wrong obligations. In rituals on the trail—in sometimes crying through those rituals—I came to a new sense of the life that lay before me and my companions: living within weaknesses—working with them—is what strength is.

Phil, Cay, and I brace against high winds on the summit of Mount Bigelow in Maine. *Nat Eddy*

In "Little Gidding," T. S. Eliot wrote: "There are three conditions which often look alike / Yet differ completely, flourish in the same hedgerow." These conditions are holding onto oneself and objects and people, letting all those things go, and indifference. Maybe not quite indifference. I was learning that I had spent the first 28 years of my life gauging my worth against outside standards, trying to get the proverbial A in life by following the rules.

One day on the trail it came to me. I was just a hiker, just another pilgrim in life. I didn't need to announce what my profession was, where I'd grown up, whom I knew, what I knew. With that realization, I could swallow the disappointment that thru-hiking was much harder than I'd imagined. I pushed on with my companions, covering too many miles. We had chosen this.

Thru-hikers represented people who on the surface looked conventional but who walked into their own eccentricities. They could be quiet thinkers, folk heroes, athletes, or amblers who cared nothing for speed or competition.

On August 30 at about 5 P.M., three days before the end of our thru-hike, I stood on the quiet white sand beach of a completely remote wilderness lake, Lower Jo-Mary Lake, deep in Maine's 100-Mile Wilderness. I tilted my filthy face toward the golden late-day sun, wanting to stop, lie down, and camp there for a week. In the background, Nat called my name. We needed to hike 1.7 miles farther to Potaywadjo Spring Lean-to. I did not want to move. But I turned and walked forward, the last steps of another day.

———————

Ultimately, it was time to go find my true voice and my children's voices in motherhood. I had not pictured myself entering a state where I could drive my writing career forward in a way that fit my particular gifts. And I began to feel the closeness of new human beings yet to be conceived. I had labored in overwork and false obligations. The AT gave me, as Eliot wrote, "a condition of complete simplicity costing not less than everything." I could see the cost of leading life from a sense of inner light instead of doing what everybody else seemed to want me to do. I saw that to say yes, I often must say no—*no* to debilitating jobs for unpleasant bosses, *no* to unreasonable demands.

I needed to provide my own sense of satisfaction and not expect it from others. But I knew that a full life is one lived in community, where each member contributes a skill, and all of the members accept one another even if they are driving them crazy.

References

Eliot, T. S. *Four Quartets* from *T. S. Eliot: The Complete Poems and Plays 1909–1950*. San Diego: Harcourt, Brace & World, 1971.

Woods, the Rev. J. C. *The Voices of Silence: Meditations on T. S. Eliot's* Four Quartets, Createspace.com, 2013.

SUMMIT NEW ENGLAND, THE MADCAP ADVENTURE

Six and a half weeks after Nat, Phil, Cay, and I reached our goal, the top of Katahdin, I started a new job in a carpeted half-acre of desk rows at *The Day*, the daily newspaper serving New London County, Connecticut. My first day there coincided with the stock market crash of October 19, 1987. The newsroom there, like most newsrooms of that time, bustled with hordes of reporters and editors cradling phones on their shoulders, punching out stories on old PC keyboards, calling out to each other. The police scanner buzzed constantly on the city desk.

I had learned of *The Day* from Dan Stets, a reporter we met in the last month of our thru-hike, while staying at Carter Notch Hut in the White Mountains. Dan had hiked in with his kids, and Nat found out he was from Philadelphia, as I was, and we got talking. I remarked that I had quit my job and we were moving to Connecticut so Nat could go back to graduate school at Yale. Dan said to call the managing editor at *The Day*. "He'll give you a job." Which he did—as a copy editor working nights. So Nat and I moved to Old Saybrook, Connecticut, midway between his school and my new paper. I loved setting out on the highway bridge in the late afternoon as the sun was dropping low over the mouth of the Connecticut River.

I'd arrive at the newsroom at its busiest time. Reporters and editors who worked first shift were turning in their stories; the night editors and the second-shift town reporters were waiting for the desks of the first-shift workers to open up.

Groups of us sat or stood around, sharing stories and fears. I did at least as much jawing about my life as I did editing others' copy in that time. The creative energy of a newsroom energized me. We hatched ideas. We teased each other. We complained together. We pushed each other to do better.

One of my coworkers was Steve Fagin, a general assignment reporter. Steve was famous at *The Day* for what he termed "madcap" adventures. One of the best was the time he was hobbling around with a broken ankle, wearing an Aircast. His wife, Lisa, cheered him up by taking him on a surprise getaway to the fancy Mount Washington Hotel. When Steve caught sight of Mount Washington rising on the horizon, he talked Lisa into climbing it that afternoon, with him in his cast. Hours later, they hobbled into the white-linen dining room, where they managed to stay awake just through the main course.

Steve and I worked different shifts and didn't overlap much, but from time to time I'd hear tales of trips he'd taken with friends, including our newsroom boss, Lance. Once, while they were climbing Mount Adams and Mount Jefferson on a fall weekend, Lance twisted his ankle on the way to Crag Camp. The sun set before they could find the camp, so they huddled in sleeping bags without tents on a muddy hillside that turned out to be within sight of the shelter.

Knowing his nonchalance for pushing himself in the backcountry, I felt no surprise one morning in spring 1999—by now I was working days as an environment reporter—when Steve stopped by my desk and asked, "Would you and Nat like to go on a madcap adventure?" He said he had been thinking about this for some time and he was sure that it was possible to climb to the top of the highest mountain in each of the six New England states in less than 48 hours.

"Less than 48 hours?" I asked. "Including driving from one to the other?"

He said yes.

I laughed. It sounded crazy. "Drive? In separate cars? Won't we be too tired to drive?"

He said we could rent an RV. He'd looked into the price and it was reasonable. "My friend Bob says he can drive us."

He had figured out a lot of details. If we climbed on the days around the summer solstice, we'd have the longest stretches of daylight and be able to minimize hiking in headlamps.

Nat and I had climbed half of the mountains involved: Katahdin in Maine, New Hampshire's Mount Washington, and Mount Greylock in Massachusetts. But we hadn't explored the imposing Mount Mansfield, which overlooked north-central Vermont, nor had we diverted ourselves to the high point in Connecticut on the shoulder of Mount Frissel. We had never even heard of the Rhode Island high point, Jerimoth Hill, in that state's northwest region. Steve said the property owner of Jerimoth Hill had closed access to the high point but that we could walk to the highway sign indicating the high point near the driveway.

I heard myself saying, "Sure, we'd love to go."

Steve named the expedition "Summit New England," organized the RV rental, and gave us instructions on where to meet up on the weekend of the summer solstice. I called my mother, who agreed to stay with our daughters for the weekend. Steve commissioned newspaper colleague Karen Ward, a page designer, to create a special logo, which he had printed on T-shirts available in two shades of green.

As we got closer to the big trek, I worried a little about my physical shape. Over the previous decade, I had been juggling raising two children with my job. Most mornings I dragged myself out of bed to run between 2 and 3 miles. That usually kept me strong enough to climb a few mountains every season. At the time, I had started backpacking with my daughters, Elizabeth and Annie, each April vacation, but those were two-day trips with low mileage. I hadn't been on a major mountain endeavor like this in years. Truth was, I worked a little too hard, drank wine most nights, and still thought life was waiting around a corner.

Summit New England would be an intense period of racing up big mountains one after the other with very little sleep. "Madcap" was a good word for it. It would stretch us a bit, but both Nat and I did have the credential of thru-hiking the AT, which, in the world of mountains, is like a master's degree. That is, Steve knew that we possessed the mental resilience and ability to stay optimistic and push through discomfort, bad weather, exhaustion, and danger.

Once we began, we'd be hiking or traveling to the next mountain around the clock—driving 2,000 miles between peaks and, as Steve calculated, trudging up 20,000 feet of elevation in between the carpooling to each trailhead. There were ten hikers—Steve, Spyros, Maggie, Phil, Tom, Ray, Brian, Skip (another friend from *The Day*), Nat, and me—plus Bob, our driver, who was also a medical doctor.

We met up at the RV in a lonely gravel parking lot in Mystic. Steve introduced me to the only other woman in our group, Maggie, an accomplished marathon runner, cyclist, and naturalist. She strode out from the RV to say hello. Her long blond hair reached the middle of her back, and she wore hiking shorts and running shoes. She looked confident, and that made me feel confident. I knew I could climb all the mountains, but I hadn't been sure how the rest of the team would find me. I didn't feel as relaxed in my own skin then as I wanted to.

We peered in the back. It held two double beds. In the front of the RV, a few sofa-like seats would work for sleeping. Seven of us started out riding in the RV, while Ray and Tom followed in their SUV.

Bob climbed into the RV's high driver's seat. Nat and I hoisted up our day packs (for when we were hiking) and duffel bags with clothes and toiletries. The engine started up. I laughed delightedly. I'd never stepped inside an RV before, let alone ridden in one, and we'd be living in this thing for two days. Bob steered us up I-395 toward northern New England. Many hours later, we pulled into a gravel parking area just outside Baxter State Park in Maine. We shared our picnic dinners while reviewing the map at the RV's little table. Nat and I slept on one of the back beds—fitfully—until 6 A.M., when we popped our heads up, boiled some coffee, and ate some snacks. Bob drove to the park entrance and rolled the vehicle into line at the gate. Soon after, we were in.

Steve said, "OK, time for a nap." We weren't going to start the clock on our six-state adventure until midday. Steve's reasoning was that if we started too early on Katahdin, the clock would be running on the adventure and we'd find ourselves on top of Mount Washington in the dark. So he said we should start to climb Katahdin in the afternoon, get down by dark, and then sleep on the way to Mount Washington in New Hampshire.

But shortly after naptime began, Steve suddenly jumped up and said, "I just realized that we can go down Washington on the auto road with our headlamps! So let's go up Katahdin right now!" We sprang up and stumbled outside of the RV. Ray and Tom, who'd parked next to us, joined the group. Steve lined us up for a photo, and we started up the trail.

Steve had chosen the shortest route to climb Katahdin, the beastly Abol Trail up the face, and I soon began to slow down and pant extra hard. Phil caught up, commented wryly that this was a little steep, and passed me and Nat. I wished I'd trained more. My T-shirt soon was soaked. But it was windless and pleasant at the top of the wide-open ridge. Skip set up his tripod. We paused a few minutes for photos and then began down the Hunt

Most of the Summit New England team on top of Katahdin. *Skip Weisenburger*

Trail, which loops around the massive face before plunging down a series of boulders. Near the bottom, Maggie suggested we jump in the stream to help our muscles. The icy water sent my brain into a still place. It was only about 1 P.M., and we'd completed our first peak. We hustled to the trailhead, where Bob was waiting for the long drive to Mount Washington.

We reached Pinkham Notch at about 5:30. The sun was low in the sky as we started up Lion Head Trail (Steve's favorite). It reaches treeline sooner than the standard route, Tuckerman Ravine Trail. Near the top, Lion Head Trail is really just a jumble of rocks that deposits hikers just below the parking lot for the auto road.

The climb in the lower reaches felt good, almost routine. As we emerged into the open and the wind picked up, I lost sight of the blazes. Spyros was just ahead. I was not sure whether we were going in the right direction. "Spy! Spy!" I called, but the wind garbled my voice, refracting it, sending it downward and away. Spy was not turning around.

I decided not to worry. Surely we were nearly there. The sun dipped low, and Nat caught up with me. We put on our headlamps as the sun finished its departure. We trudged onto the asphalt around to a utility building, peeked inside, and there sat the rest of the group, bundled up, reclining against the walls.

"At least she's still smiling," Phil said.

Then we walked 7 miles down the auto road in the dark, the most endless walking I've ever done. The road switchbacked around and around. Nat and I brought up the rear. The others were a few tenths of a mile ahead of us, and we followed the slight flares their headlamps made in the sky. Near the bottom, lightning bugs, maybe the first of the season, put on a show for our weary eyes. Finally, we rounded one last bend and saw the tiny lights of a couple of parked vehicles in the giant gravel lot below. Way in the distance, by the road, the RV waited. It was after midnight.

Inside, we stretched out, taking turns on the beds and cushioned seats. We'd lie down, start snoozing, and then the RV would hit a bump. Our bodies would go flying a foot into the air and then plop back onto the mattresses and chairs.

Three hours later, we rose from our roller-coaster naps; laced on our shoes; hoisted our backpacks with snacks, extra clothing, water, and first aid; and set out up the Long Trail to the top of Mount Mansfield. Lightning bugs blinked in front of me as I followed the others. Within an hour, a beautifully sunny morning sent rays down through the forest canopy. Once again, the faster group—everyone but Skip, Nat, and me—went ahead.

I reached the top of Mount Mansfield just after sunrise. The faster hikers were napping.

Near the top, I encountered a crazy-steep boulder up which I had to scramble to reach the summit ridge. I'd gotten ahead of Nat and Skip and needed to tackle it on my own.

"Come *on*," I said to myself. And just pushed up. Scary as it was, I did not think to wait for Nat. I just kept moving and reached the rest of the group, all resting on the sunny rocks. They jumped up, smiling, as soon as Nat and Skip reached us, and soon enough we began trotting down. The rest of the day was a bit of a blur. Bob parked near one of the access trails to Greylock, which would be a short trot from a trail that intersected the auto road up the mountain. We climbed the tower on the summit, at which point my fear of heights took hold of me. My legs shook, I became dizzy, and the moving light on either side of the spiral staircase terrified me.

But soon enough, we tumbled back into our vehicles, and by late afternoon of the second day, we were trotting up the side of forested Mount Frissell. Its top rises in Massachusetts, but Connecticut's highest point is on its shoulder. We sat in a little grove of young trees to rest and eat snacks. Steve stood up to make a speech: Did a madcap summit scramble qualify as a great athletic endeavor? We interrupted him with our laughter. Of course it did, but we weren't going to puff ourselves up about it.

He left it at "Hey everyone, I know we're going to succeed. This has meant a lot to me." A few hours later, we trotted the final yards up the side of Route 101 in Foster, Rhode Island, where a green Department of Transportation sign marked the nearest legal access to Jerimoth Hill, just a few thousand feet away. We'd done it! Summited New England.

What did I learn? That I was not as fast as some others but that I still had a lot of fire in me. That the faster athletes had pulled me to places I'd missed without them. I cherished the bonds with them because I had become half an athlete and half a philosopher, and now I felt fully both.

VERTIGO

As a kid running from one amusement ride to another on the boardwalk in Ocean City, I felt no fear. I'd laugh while "The Scrambler," which looked like a giant insect with chairs, would throw us around. My favorite for a while was a tilting disc called "Around the World," which attached riders' bodies to the side of a roundabout by centrifugal force as it whirled, angling gradually to an upright. My brother John and I rode this thing twice one night, just before the boardwalk closed. After the ride slowed to a halt, we ran along the weathered boards. Leaped, really.

Childhood is like that. Free, unselfconscious. Then I began to grow into a woman. Taller, with insulating layers and wider hips and a curved waist. I didn't like the feeling. My body grew as nature meant it to grow, although by age 17 I wished I could remain lithe and unaware of physical limitations, the way I'd once felt as a champion mile runner. But now my body moved through the world differently. I didn't know how to feel free, how to leap around the way I always had. I stood with my arms crossed in front of me, cautious and self-conscious.

One June evening near the end of my junior year of high school, some friends and I carpooled to the boardwalk in Pleasantville. Without thinking, I lined up with my ticket for the salt-and-pepper-shaker ride and climbed on, smiling. I was back at the shore, getting on the rides as I had done so many times. But soon it started swinging us up and down, and the pavement and crowds and little snack shack buildings and other rides all became blurry and whooshed by upside down. Oh God, I wanted to be out of there, but we were hanging upside down far above the boardwalk. Can someone feel both confined and recklessly tossed into the air at the same time? That's how it seemed. I screwed my eyes shut and held my breath. I was panicking. Our car and the car opposite ours hung upside down for many seconds. A girl in the other car screamed, "AAAAAAAAH, isn't this great?" Then she paused and I heard her voice directed at me: "You don't look so good."

After that, as long as my feet were on the ground, I felt safe. I climbed mountains, scrambled up rocks. But high ladders, balconies with low railings, and skyscraper windows sent my vision into a fog. Ascending circular stairs in old stone towers made sweat pop out on my nose. My legs would go half-numb and start shaking. I didn't react that way on mountains, unless the cliffs were especially steep or the ridges had knife edges, and on the Appalachian Trail, I had learned how to butt-slide or look only up as I scrambled.

I met vertigo full on in June 2003, the third day of a five-day backpacking trip in the High Peaks region of New York's Adirondack Mountains. I was 44. My friends Bob (a different Bob than our RV driver in the previous chapter), Skip, Bob's 13-year-old daughter, Zoe, my 13-year-old daughter, Annie, and I lugged our full packs, each weighing about 40 pounds, through trails littered with fallen trees. The mountains were rock domes. One morning we dragged ourselves up Basin Mountain, which resembled an upside-down basin. Near the top, an especially high, scary ledge demanded we pull ourselves up. I perched on the narrow shelf of rock searching out a crack I could curl my fingers into. I was shaking and started to cry. Even in my fear, I felt ashamed. I should lead my daughter; instead, here I stood blubbering like a ninny. What had happened to me in the years since my Appalachian Trail thru-hike when I'd pulled myself up and butt-slid down hundreds of ledges?

Annie works her way down a ladder below a blown-down tree in the Adirondacks.

Skip leaned down, extending his hand. "Come on, Chris," he said, "you can do this." He tugged my wrist and I pushed down with one foot and used one knee to get up. I could not look into that void behind me. On the summit, I mustered a smile as a hiker agreed to take a picture of our group. Behind us, the mountains unfolded in pleated layers of slate and deeper blues.

We walked to the edge of Basin's dome and prepared to sink down the steep trail into the col between it and the next peak, Mount Saddleback. We stood just before the trail dropped off, staring across to Saddleback's white rock face glowing in the midday sun. Tiny, dark shapes moved on that pale surface. Like ants.

Someone asked, "Are those people?" That could not be. I did not see that! We started down into the trees. About 45 minutes later, we began to claw our way out of the forest onto the rock. The weight of my gear pulled on my shoulders as if to pry me backward off the face. My little tantrum on Basin Mountain receded into quaint memory. Now we stood with full packs below an open rock face, really a technical climb. We carried no ropes, no carabiners. We knew nothing of bouldering or free climbing. Dread surrounded me like a cloud, a very subtle cloud, really just droplets that make one blink because it seems the cloud isn't there at all. Terror that immense could not be grasped. I could not imagine going farther up. Nor could I envision retreating. I felt trapped.

We scrambled to a ledge high on that giant rock face, with nowhere farther to go—it seemed. We could see holes and stubs of metal rods where handholds had once helpfully steadied adventurers. Now there were none. The rock sloped alarmingly to a horizon above my forehead. The summit lay beyond that.

Bob and Skip frowned. "Let's scout this without our packs and come back," Skip said. They both dropped their gear at my feet and scrambled up an impossibly steep piece of rock in front of us. The girls and I were left standing there. I realized that I had no choice but to be a better mother to Annie and a calmer leader to Zoe.

"Girls, let's think of our favorite cakes," I said.

An eerie calm had inhabited them. I filled the air with my chatter. "I really like chocolate cake with white icing, but I also will eat chocolate cake with chocolate icing," I said. All of us sat down, leaning back against the rock wall and keeping our feet from the edge. The brilliant sun and warm breeze signaled a perfect mountain day. I had never, ever, seen a trail that navigated a steep face like this. Nothing on the AT could rival it. But I wondered if it were just that my hiking brain had gone rusty over the last fifteen years and I had forgotten why mountains are mountains. In any case, I had to stay calm for Annie and Zoe. We were not turning around and going back the way we came. We were going to go up.

Suddenly, Skip appeared from the left. How had he gotten to us that way? He was alone. He said, "OK, I'm going to pass my pack up to Bob and then Bob's pack." We looked straight above us and could see Bob's boots and Bob's legs. Skip grunted and held his pack as high as he could and handed it to Bob. I watched as the pack slithered precariously up and away. They repeated this with Bob's pack. Annie's pack. Zoe's. Mine. Then Bob disappeared again.

Skip addressed the girls, assuming, I knew, that I would be all right (apparently trusting me not to fall apart): "Annie, Zoe, we're going to do a traverse. The rock is dry. Your boots will stay on it, like this." Adrenaline no doubt fueled him to do what he did next. He took three or four running steps up the steep face and then ran down backward. Just to demonstrate. He did not slip. He did it a few times more. I could see he wanted us to realize that he did not slip. "See? You will stay on the rock. Now we're going to hold hands. We're doing to do a traverse. There's an easier place to get you up. Now, everybody hold hands."

Speechless, I cooperated, feigning calm.

"One, two, three, go!" Skip said, and we were suddenly walking across the cliff, holding hands. He did not really drag us so much as pull, and I did not dare let out a squeak. Our boots stayed on the slanting rock. Skip led us to a place about 20 yards along the face. "This spot is easier to get up." Its rough surface gave us little bumps to grab onto. A wide crack bisected part of it. Bob stood above.

The girls went first. Zoe scrambled up the crack as Skip steadied her from behind and Bob grabbed her hand and pulled her up. Then Annie went, and I followed. Skip soon joined us, navigating the crack for the second time that day.

Unbelievable! We were up that face. We had followed the people who from Basin had looked like ants on the rock face. Now we trudged over to a wide, flat, open area: the top. I felt as if we were the only climbers left in

Saddleback Mountain, with the cliffs on the left, in the Adirondacks High Peaks. *Wikimedia Commons/CC BY 3.0*

the world. We sat down and pulled out our lunch bags. I could not focus on the multitude of mountains laid out in all directions before us. I sighed. We had gotten up that ledge!

A young man emerged over the lip of the cliff. He loped up to us and then kind of bounced by, commenting, "Isn't this fantastic?"

Many weeks later, Bob told me a story. He and Skip had started up the wide crack on the cliff. The guidebook described this route as "steep." A few years before, it said, trail maintainers had removed old metal cables. Bob's foot got stuck in the crack. Trying to pull his foot out, he clutched the rock and wriggled the foot back and forth. Over and over. Suddenly, he said, he felt a strange push of energy, and his foot seemed to just fly out of the crack. He raced the rest of the way up behind Skip.

After we returned home, Bob learned that at precisely the moment his foot had come free, his best friend had died bicycling. A pickup truck hit him from behind as he pedaled along a state road in Connecticut. Bob insisted that something had happened out there to help him up the rock, and he believed it was related to his friend, who had climbed many mountains with him. He told me that his friend had almost come with us on the trip, but changed his mind.

The cliff scare transformed me too: I stopped fearing heights. Vertigo—technically, acrophobia—had felt like a monster I could never control. Now, on that cliff, I'd gone through what doctors would call exposure therapy. I had to deal with the cliff. I had to stay calm for the girls. I had to control feelings I'd thought I could not control.

Back home, my fear of heights was gone. And I mean, *gone.* I first realized it while reporting a story for *The Day* on the ferry between New London, Connecticut, and Port Jefferson, Long Island. The first mate showed me around when I boarded and invited me to meet the captain on the bridge.

I looked up at the metal ladder and its open-air rungs and wondered how violently my legs would shake. But I had a column to write. I *had* to speak to the captain. I prepared for a miserable ascent up the ladder, hoping I'd get to the door before my eyes fogged up, but as I started to climb, something was different. It felt exciting, like childhood on the "Around the World" ride. I looked around, enjoying the view, the wind, the waves way down below. I thought, "Aren't I usually terrified of this kind of thing?" No, I was not afraid. Did I obsess on my new bravery and begin to get scared again? No. That sensation of falling into a panic hole, losing my battle of the wills, had vanished. Spending so much time on the steep side of Mount Saddleback had jolted my brain out of this phobia. I must keep on top of it or the fear would return. Exposure to heights makes tall places seem normal; to avoid tall places would nurture my fear. So I knew that I would conquer vertigo by stepping to the edge of the places where it had resided in me. The mountains, again, would restore my equilibrium, as long as I kept going back.

"ECHO, ECHO"

Fifteen people had crammed sleeping bags onto the floor of the Guyot Shelter deep in the White Mountains that wet August night. The structure's open front faced rows of dark pines. I stood on the platform edge, staring into the light curtain of rain. All around, stoves hissed, sleeping bags zipped, spoons clanged against pots. I had just given the rest of my extra stove fuel to a guy who'd settled into the only chair, a seat hewn out of an old stump and propped at the edge of the platform.

The man said he had deliberately *not* brought enough fuel. "I'm out for ten days," he said. "My stove holds enough fuel for nine meals. This is the eighth meal. I don't carry extra fuel, to save weight."

Someone said, "I have some extra fuel, if you need it."

He didn't answer. He stared out at the rain, stroking his long, dark hair. And then he started a monologue.

"This strange thing happened the other night," he said. "I was on the Davis Path, staying at the Resolution Shelter." (This was in 2002, a decade before the Appalachian Mountain Club's backcountry crew finally tore down that shelter in the federal Wilderness Area.) The Resolution Shelter was named after a forested mountain few visitors seek out—Mount Resolution. The peak honors the resolve of Nathaniel Davis, a nineteenth-century trail builder who graded a 15-mile bridle path to the top of Mount Washington. The Davis Path is a lonelier route than most others in that area.

The stranger continued, "I'm more afraid of humans than I am of anything else in the woods. There was a guy out in the dark somewhere nearby. I couldn't see him. But he kept calling out to me as if he wanted me to answer him. He had amazing skills, because he never showed himself. He kept calling out: 'Yodel! Yodel! Yodel! Echo! Echo!' I ignored him for a long time. But then I answered him in a tiny voice, 'Echo.' He just kept yelling out those words over and over.

"I sat there until about 8 o'clock, listening to this," he said. "Then I decided to pack up and leave for the next shelter."

He said he had no headlamp or flashlight, just a little 2-inch-long pen-light, the sort you buy at a convenience store and affix to a key ring. He was holding that light as he told the story, and he flicked it on for a second with his thumb.

"I kept thinking that someone without my skills could have slipped and hit his head on a rock," he said, "but I got out onto the trail and made pretty good time going 2 miles." He thought he heard someone following along aside him, off the path, but he wasn't sure.

I shifted to the other foot but did not move away. A few of the men were listening with one ear, it seemed, as they went about the business of putting away their gear for the night. But I, the only woman at the shelter that night, listened attentively. I ran over in my mind what he was saying. It didn't quite make sense—packing up after dark and hiking out right past the unseen intruder to escape him.

At the next shelter (which must have been the now-torn-down Rocky Branch Shelter Number 1), he said, "I spent a fitless night." He must have meant "fitful," but I suppressed the urge to correct him, smiling into the dark as he went on.

"I didn't know where the guy was. He had to be out there, waiting. My friends ask me if I'm afraid of bears. I say I worry most about humans." He flicked the penlight.

I have debated with myself since then whether the man made up the whole thing and he himself had been the yodeler. In which case I was politely hanging out with a creep while the other campers used some sixth sense and avoided him.

I believe that I am an expert in most backpacking skills and that I can take care of myself in the woods. The rape and murder rates in remote areas (about 300 over a period of five years in the national parks, for example) don't come close to those on city streets (428 per 100,000 people in 2011, the FBI reports). But this storyteller, whether truthful or not, made my land-scape feel creepier that night. He may have done it for his own ego. And I stood by his tree-stump-chair throne giving him an audience.

Every few years, I review that experience. I sit on my own chair, star-ing out into my own woods, wondering about the man who escaped the yodeling stalker. Assuming he told the truth, his story made me think more

Clouds battle with sun in early morning at Guyot Shelter.

about those unlikely dangers. But if the man at Guyot Shelter lied, then I encouraged his fraudulent bravery by listening for so long. Maybe he was just trying to impress the only woman at the shelter. Perhaps he could not perceive awe in the forest just by considering the surroundings. He had to invent a mystery.

I encountered him one more time, the next evening. My friends Steve and Tom and I were crossing Franconia Brook near Thirteen Falls after a long day and were eager to set up our tents at the campsite. There, coming the other way, was the man who'd told the story the previous night. He wore navy-blue rain pants, although it was a dry evening, and he carried nothing. "I was looking for the water," he said mysteriously, although he had no water bottles or pump. He walked on.

I never saw him again. He wasn't at the campsite. Perhaps he was camping in the woods away from the tent platforms. Or maybe he wanted to speed-hike through the night and escape intruders—real or imaginary.

Part II

THE GIRLS

The All-Girl Quest, 1997–2003

NEW HAMPSHIRE
2003: Greenleaf Hut, Mount Lafayette, Garfield Ridge Trail, Galehead Hut, Gale River Trail

VIRGINIA
1998: Pine Mountain, Wilburn Ridge, Grayson Highlands Area (1)

1999: McAfee Knob, Lamberts Meadow Shelter (2)

2000: Bald Knob, Cow Camp Gap Shelter, Cole Mountain (3)

TENNESSEE
1997: Grassy Ridge near Carvers Gap, Appalachian Trail, side trail

2001: Attempted Grassy Ridge

2002: Successful trip to Grassy Ridge: Carvers Gap to Overmountain Shelter to Wildermine Campsite

The All-Girl Quest

One evening in October 1996, I was picking up dishes and old papers in my kitchen. My daughter Elizabeth stood by the tiny doorway to the dining room. "A boy at school said girls are weak," she announced.

"What?" I screeched. "That's not true." I shook my head. Ugh, hadn't my generation already sorted out this misinformation? Where was this boy's mother? Had the world evolved at all since Title IX?

I began my best equality speech: "Girls are strong. Maybe you're not exactly as strong as he is, but strong." Life is not a competition. Strength is often an attitude.

I had heard the same on the playgrounds of my childhood. My friends and I had actually enjoyed a game that later seemed creepy: Boys captured the girls as if we were helpless. They'd grab hold of our arms and lead us like zoo animals back to an imaginary holding pen in the trees that lined the blacktop. We went willingly, as if we were prizes they owned. I never tried to escape. I was 8. What did I know?

I did not mention this to Elizabeth. I just said that the boy had not told her the truth and she should not believe it. I wondered whether boys had primal urges to exert power. I'd been wondering this most of my life. I loved the energy of boys, having grown up with three older brothers, yet the playground and its rituals of power seemed unchanged since my childhood. Kids are forever on their own in that freewheeling environment. What could I say that would help Elizabeth navigate this? I wanted to help her and her younger sister, Annie, gain confidence in the playgrounds of the world.

I worried that such misguided declarations could become part of how they viewed themselves. On playgrounds, adults rarely overheard comments and rarely understood context. Teachers told us parents in the 1990s that we should "grab a teachable moment." Here came mine in the kitchen. I took up my mantle, determined that I could inspire my daughters to be feminists through scrambling uphill. This was the genesis of seven all-girl backpacking trips during spring vacation.

After she had grown up and was on her way to becoming a nurse, Elizabeth told me she didn't remember this stunning moment in the kitchen, but she did remember boys telling her that girls shouldn't be scientists. She thought her father and I had probably taught her that girls are not weaklings: "I definitely experienced implicitly and explicitly boys saying girls shouldn't do/shouldn't be good at science, but, luckily, had also been inoculated against that by you guys, especially Deed." (Deed is Nat, her father.)

She also said, "I do feel that the way you and Deed split up household tasks, which was not the 'traditional' mom does all cooking/cleaning/child-rearing and dad mows the lawn, played a strong role in letting me discard limiting ideas about what girls and women could and couldn't do."

After Annie had grown up, she reported that the boys she knew in childhood tended to put out a double message. On the one hand, they would say, "Girls are disgusting." On the other, they believed (Annie said) that "girls can do everything, so it's OK to punch them, and they ought to have to register for the draft." As if equality would blow up in girls' faces.

As far as I knew and my daughters remembered, they hadn't devoted time arguing with boys about this. They found ways to work around it. Walked away, perhaps.

At that moment in the kitchen, I looked down at my young daughter and understood that raising girls offered me a challenge. I mentally filed the problem as an action call.

———

It had been nearly ten years since Nat and I had hiked the Appalachian Trail with our friends Cay and Phil. I was still laboring on a book manuscript about that trip. I took my early chapters to writers' conferences only to come away discouraged that my long journey could hold meaning for a wider audience. Writers I admired, and those who were students next to me at those conferences, told me not to give away that we had made it to Katahdin—but so many outdoor stories start out with the ending. I felt misunderstood and dismissed. I thought of our AT hike as a snappy tale of the woes and triumphs of an ordinary woman. I had whined, cried, and felt hopeless many days, but I had continued trudging. By about Massachusetts, I moved on the instinct of a new life and stopped caring what people thought of me.

A writer at one workshop agreed to look at some of my pages. She said, "Don't start crying until halfway through the book." But I was more of a crier than that. Still, her point resonated. I did not know yet how best to tell the story. Writing is a lifelong journey full of tough lessons. Just like the trail.

Now I was becoming obsessed with what people (writers at conferences, editors at work, strangers in the community) thought of me. I felt overwhelmed with full-time newspaper reporting, running from town hall to police station to zoning meeting. I was working on a proposal to become my paper's part-time environment writer so that I could start doing some freelancing. I didn't think the paper would allow me to write about the environment full time. Still, the potential for a shift in my work thrilled me. And scared me.

I called my friend Jenifer one day, and we talked a long time—mostly about the way my parents had been disorganized and somewhat chaotic, as wonderful as they were. My father was a self-made man whose parents had divorced in the 1930s. That background had left a few demons in him. My mother had never been on time, and her habits of molding the minutes and hours to match her desires were ingrained in me. I worried I was creating chaos in my mind and in my routines out of habit. Taking on too much and working too hard made me feel more alive and yet also more confined. Jen told me she could relate to some of what I said. My situation was not unusual; the antidote was to take better care of myself. I needed to regain the way I had felt on the Appalachian Trail. I needed the trail the way a sick person needs oxygen.

Most mornings, I slid out of bed before Nat left for his teaching job and went for my run before the girls woke up. These road jaunts took me past a craggy ledge and oak-dominated forest overlooking a shallow pond. Often, checking my watch, I'd turn around at a red house called Tumble Hill Farm and spring back past the pond, down the hill, avoiding slippery piles of acorns at the road's edge. I'd huff up a slight rise as the houses thickened again, take a final left turn at the stop sign, and sprint home.

Some days I ran my "milk route"—literally, on days we were out of milk. Instead of turning toward the ledge and the oak trees, I'd go straight at that stop sign, to the end of West Bridge Street, turn left onto Route 80, run straight into town, buy milk at the little supermarket, and then walk or jog home with the gallon jug sloshing.

Days when I didn't feel I had time to run at all seemed never to start, as if I hadn't ever awakened. But lately even on some days when I did go running, I felt confined at sea level. I could not find myself. I was not at peace in my own body.

So I began to plan a camping trip in the southern Appalachians. My daughters' April vacation was coming up. Nat's private school closed for break in March, and by April, he was back at work. That meant that the trip would be an all-female adventure. I began reading the AT guidebooks, looking for an exciting two- to three-day backpacking route, something challenging, big. I would teach my girls about self-sufficiency through going from Point A to Point B in the southern Appalachians. I hoped they would find it a little hard but not too tough, just enough to see what they were capable of. The lessons for them would be incredible, but the deep reason I was planning this was my own hiking fever.

I was doing it for them and doing it for myself, the way great explorers have throughout history. "Sometimes science is the excuse for exploration. I think it is rarely the reason," George Mallory told an audience in 1923, before he set out for Mount Everest. Sometimes teaching self-sufficiency is the excuse for exploration, I could say.

I wanted to instill my daughters with physical confidence and teach them how it creates mental confidence and a sense of purpose in the world. These girls could inhabit wild places for a while. I would take them into the southern Appalachians for a few days, where we would sleep in our tent, cook outside, carry water, and walk through whatever weather came. I was trying to recreate in a few days the major growth I'd experienced in four and a half months on the AT.

People can't live permanently on mountaintops—or at least they shouldn't. But I knew from my own experience that I could move through them for a few days, weeks, or months, until I became accustomed to that place where nothing resembles home, where survival requires movement and planning, and where discomfort and pain become normal annoyances necessary to live among wild animals, stunning views, and rock ledges.

My lesson plan for spring break with the girls was: learn to feel uncomfortable, set up a tent, walk through rain, cook over a white gas stove while leaning over a dirty platform. Then, back in civilization, if smoke entered a building and they had to run down the stairs, or if a hurricane snuffed out the electricity for a week, they could deal with those events. They would understand that a satisfying life is not about seeking only comfort and ease.

At least, that was the plan.

RAGE ON GRASSY RIDGE

To my list of fears—the dark, strange dogs, wasps, and ladders—I added a dread of thunderstorms after the night of April 22–23, 1997. Elizabeth, Annie, and I spent that night inside a tent while thunder, winds, and rain whipped across the open saddle below Grassy Ridge Bald, which stands at more than 6,000 feet in the Appalachian Mountains at the Tennessee–North Carolina border.

The gray clouds rolling in that evening did not look threatening, and it was not cold when we left, but the temperature dipped as the storm thrust in to meet our campsite. Long stretches of rough wind and driving rain hit between about midnight and dawn. I stayed awake most of that time trying to stop the tent from swaying. I stretched my arms into a beam to hold up the tent while the storm lashed from the northwest at a 45-degree angle against the nylon.

Going into that night, I had slept in a tent in the Appalachian Mountains between northern Georgia and central Maine about 45 times and in trailside shelters at least 80 times. I'd never seen rain like this. In spring 1987, the year Nat, Phil, Cay, and I had hiked the entire Appalachian Trail, we trudged through daily afternoon thunderstorms for about ten days. During one deluge, lightning ripped open a tree a quarter-mile north of where I huddled with Cay. At the crash of electricity destroying the tree trunk, I practically jumped into her arms. A moment later, we started hiking again and passed the giant shards strewn down the forested incline. I wasn't scared, just impressed. I liked thunderstorms. I relished the sweet smell of a downpour that breaks long days of strangling heat.

I had driven more than 800 miles to the grassy highlands of Tennessee and North Carolina from our house in central Connecticut to make reality out of an idle dream. "Did you know there are mountains with just grass growing on top?" I had asked Elizabeth and Annie, ages 8 and 6, one night as I was putting them to bed. One of them said, "I want to see them." "I'll take you there someday," I promised.

When we got to Carver's Gap, the girls galloped away from the car while I put the last things in my pack. It was after 5 p.m. The mountain was just as I'd advertised. A neat mound of grass rose impressively into scuttling light-gray clouds and patches of late afternoon sun.

A woman and two children hiked down toward us as we made our way up Round Bald. The half-hidden sun was at our backs, and, to the right, greenish clouds drifted slowly from south to north.

"Are you camping out?" the grandmotherly woman said, smiling. She and the children were finishing their adventure for the day. Did she think we were imprudent to set out with those clouds rolling in? I was used to walking through all kinds of weather. I did not tell Annie and Elizabeth that the radio announcer had droned on about a "one hundred percent chance of rain tonight and tomorrow." We were still an hour from our mountain when I heard that. Weather is regional and changeable, and forecasts in the East often can't stay ahead of what ultimately happens. I like to gamble on the optimistic side. (The announcer also said nothing about thunder.)

"Yes," I replied, and we smirked at one another as mothers do in public. Our expressions said we both knew how hard it is to get children out on a hike. I was weighted down with most of the gear, which was stuffed into the same sea-green North Face pack I'd been using for ten years. My girls carried their own clothes in their school packs, which each also held a tiny spiral notepad and pencil to use for drawing and writing and a tiny flashlight. They wore whistles on nylon cords around their necks.

The hike started out straight to the east, beyond a fence and over a stile, going up stone steps through the turf, which still was dead though this was the beginning of spring. Within fifteen minutes we were sitting on a large rock eating peanut M&Ms. We continued our gentle climb to the highest part of Round Bald, the first peak, which was not much higher than the road. "Look, girls," I kept saying, admiring the expanse on either side. The grass reached away to air and clouds on all sides.

The balds don't want to stay that way naturally. The government care-takers of Pisgah National Forest have brought in sheep at times to maintain the openness. Our dream ridge hadn't been wild for long: within a half-mile we walked through a shallow depression between peaks that's called Engine Gap after an abandoned sawmill engine. A little farther along the path, a sign marked Jane Bald, a mountain named after the victim of a terrible tragedy. A woman died there of milk sickness. She got the disease from the milk of a cow that had eaten poisonous snakeroot. This ridge was the site of the highest farm east of the Rockies until the mid-1960s.

The trail forked. We could go left to stay on the Appalachian Trail, 1.4 miles more to a three-sided Appalachian Trail shelter, or we could head about a half-mile south to a grassy campsite with a spring nearby. My plan was for us to head on the left fork the next day. For tonight, I'd picked the route to the right, which led to the closer campsite with no shelter. My desire was always to stay one step ahead of my children's complaining—to get them to something beautiful in a few miles.

We turned right. In minutes, without climbing much at all, we were at the highest open peak in the Southern Appalachians (others have trees or buildings on top), a lonely meadow full of alder. I high-stepped through some of this undergrowth to make sure it was our campsite and found the plaque honoring farmers who used to live there.

It was still partially sunny when the ridge rolled down into a little col. "This is it," I said. The girls came to life—hurled down their packs and grabbed their notebooks. They perched on a giant rock at the edge of an undergrowth of rhododendrons and drew pictures of the grass, the few trees jutting up, the rocks framing distant ridges, and of me, pulling out the gear.

I began to taste the fear of full responsibility as I struggled with the tent. The outer layer, the fly, wasn't quite right. This was a tent I hadn't put up in several years. We had two others we used more often, but this was bigger. I jammed the metal pins in and the fly hung askew but covered the entrance flap. As soon as it was up the girls jumped inside and settled into their sleeping bags.

I reached into the pack for the food bag. The girls were chattering away, so I decided to quietly slip away down the eastern slope to fill up the nylon water bag. At the spring in a tenth of a mile, a PVC pipe neatly routed the water over rocks. I squatted for a few minutes in the dusky light, holding the bag's opening under the pipe. When I got back to the campsite it was raining lightly, and the girls were standing outside the tent in their stocking feet. "What are you doing out in the rain in your socks?" I panted as I lugged the water up to them.

They darted toward me and cried out, "Mama!" My heart lurched. I'd scared them by disappearing without saying anything. "I didn't know if I should blow my whistle," Annie said. Her emergency whistle was in case she was lost. I felt terrible but hid it beneath briskness. "OK, well, go back inside the tent, and I'll have spaghetti ready in a minute." The air was going gray, and misty rain continued to sift downward.

I pumped the little lever on the gas stove and got it going. The pot boiled, the spaghetti cooked in its lump in my battered camping pot. I tore open the sauce mix envelope and wrenched open the little can of tomato paste. I stirred everything up and took the whole pot in to the girls. I barely had time to be grateful for the hot meal that makes camping sweet when the rain began to pour and thunder crashed.

"I'm sad," Elizabeth said, with little emotion. It sounded like an announcement. Annie let loose with, "I'm scared, Mama!" She cried as the lightning flashed.

I was also scared. I knew that lightning strikes the highest thing, and there we were on an open ridge in a tent with metal poles. The guidebooks say tents are as dangerous as convertible cars at a time like this. Still, I comforted myself by recalling the couple of pines near us that were higher targets.

Then the lightning and thunder were only about a second apart, and I said, "Say a prayer." Annie started wailing again. *Why did I say that?* I thought. Elizabeth sat silent at my left. I reached inward for control.

"Girls, there are two mountains on either side of us. They'll protect us from the lightning. We are going to be OK," I said.

What I didn't say was my fear of what would happen if the lightning happened to be exactly where we were. I felt this sickening panic, an urge to jump out of the tent and start running in any direction. Then I thought of how dark it was now, and I tried to modulate my breathing and remain calm. I'm not usually a calm person in an emergency. When my husband fell against a razor-sharp tree branch and cut open his head on Baldpate Mountain in Maine, it was Cay who bandaged him up while I stood with my back to the scene, muttering, "Oh my God."

———

The storm raged for two distinct periods. First the thunder crashed and rain poured straight onto us for about two hours, from perhaps 9 to 11 P.M. I had no watch. During this time, I decided we weren't bothering to brush our teeth and would just go to sleep. It was so loud that I yelled the nightly prayer, "NOW I *LAY ME DOWN* TO *SLEEP* . . ." Then I sang whatever hymns I could remember. Elizabeth hummed with me. I reached into the girls' packs for their raincoats to cover the sleeping bags, in case water dripped in. But Annie had no raincoat.

The afternoon in the car came back to me: *"Mama, I can't fit my raincoat."*
"Don't worry, Annie, I'll help you with it when we get to the trail."

So I pulled out my waterproof pack cover and put that on top of her. Both girls rolled over and, by some miracle, fell asleep.

I sat up through this first deluge. When it stopped, I peeked outside of the tent flap. Behind the clouds, the moon's light filtered through the fog. It was dead quiet. I went outside to relieve myself, and I thought how beautiful the surroundings were right now. Still, I was tense. I crawled back inside and lay down, thinking that maybe we'd be dry enough in the morning to continue on 3 miles northeast to the Overmountain Shelter. Under a good roof it wouldn't matter how much it rained.

Then came the second hell. I had no idea what time it was—maybe 1 A.M. This time there was no thunder or lightning, just a driving wind and rain. The wind whistled as the tent walls swayed back and forth, and long bursts of loud, spattering rain pelted the fabric. Sitting up between the girls, I felt very lonely. Although Elizabeth was also awake, she didn't say anything. My feet were a little damp, the sleeping bag was heavy with the water it had soaked up, and I kept pulling my girls' limp bodies away from the little rivulets of water at the side.

It was then I knew we weren't going to the Overmountain Shelter in the morning. We were going to march straight back to the car. But how would we see through the fog? Then I recalled that the trails through the balds were chiseled deep in the meadow grass, actually trenches a few feet deep. We couldn't get lost.

Ages later, the rain lightened up and finally stopped. I lay down and almost dozed off, until I could tell the sun was up. I crawled outside, glad to be OK, disappointed that my camping trip was disintegrating before my eyes, and worried the stove wouldn't light. But I had kept both the stove and the matches inside their Ziploc bag in my pack next to me, and the flame roared. I was not a vigilant cook this morning. The Cream of Wheat congealed into a giant lump.

The girls suited up silently, leaving me to eat most of the cereal, which made me retch. They stood around while I dismantled the sagging tent. My hands seized up as I tried to pull out the pins and stuff the sopping mess of fabric into the sack. Behind me, Annie looked lost inside my gigantic

After a miserable night, the all-girl hiking trip about-faced and hiked back to the car instead of continuing to another campsite. Annie and I pause in the fog on Round Bald. *Elizabeth Eddy*

raincoat. "My hands are cold," she wailed. "WAAAAAAAAH." Elizabeth just stood there.

I marched around, jamming stuff into my pack. The frying pan I'd bought at a pharmacy somewhere in Virginia to cook pancakes would not fit, so I set it by the cooking rock. Annie angrily took off my raincoat, said it was too big, and handed it back to me. I faced my grim charges and announced, "OK, let's go. Just keep walking. You can't stop this morning. You'll get cold. We're going to keep going. You can do it."

"YEEEEEEEEEEEUH," Annie wept as she stepped up out of the col through the mud in her high-top sneakers, pajamas, shorts, and fleece jacket with tiny drops all over its fuzz.

"Let's count the flowers, girls," I said desperately. We were going to start counting the tiny bluets—the wildflowers in the turf—on the way out, and I guessed there would be ten. I was thinking how hikers usually get into trouble just when they think they're out of it. They get hurt going down a mountain, for instance, or they get lost and sometimes die within a mile of civilization.

We counted more than 400 bluets. Annie stopped crying and laughed at me because I'd thought there would only be ten. We even pulled out the disposable camera and snapped shots of each other along the ridge.

Eighteen months after this happened, I set out to document the violent weather we'd survived. What did I find? This incident, which proved I could not recognize thunderclouds at high elevations and which tested my ability to care for my children, was an ordinary storm.

Even the temperature was not remarkable. It hit the low 40s overnight (about 10 degrees below the usual). The bursts of rain after midnight, which resembled the angry hand of God to me, measured less than an inch. In Asheville, North Carolina, about 48 miles southwest of our campsite, roughly three-quarters of an inch was recorded on the 22nd, while on the 23rd, a half-inch. In Bristol, Tennessee, about 32 miles north of our tent, a fraction of an inch fell on the 22nd, and between midnight the 23rd and through that next day, only three-fifths of an inch.

Fractions of an inch had taken me to the edge of my courage. I recalled trying to sing an old Quaker hymn, only bits of the words coming back to me: "My life goes on in endless song, above Earth's lamentation . . . No storm can shake my inmost calm, while to that rock I'm clinging . . ." For miles in either direction, there were no humans but us, sometimes forgetting to breathe inside our little swaying tent. It was too dark to see if my daughters were peering at me with trust or terror. But we all pretended we could handle it . . . and we did.

Spring in the southern mountains brings unsettled weather, wintry cold, and sometimes tragedy—people expect it. On the 18th, most of western North Carolina seized up under a freeze that damaged apple orchards. The evening before our night on Grassy Ridge, a storm raged through eastern Tennessee and much of North Carolina, with hailstones as large as golf balls, while a "short line segment convection"—a wind formation—roared east-northeast from Georgia to South Carolina, knocking over trees and power lines and damaging 46 buildings.

The day after our trial, a red oak tree in central Tennessee was struck by lightning, and weather observers said chunks of wood 75 pounds apiece flew 50 yards through the air. A piece of tree got embedded in the taillight of a car, and the lightning dug a trench almost 3 feet deep along the tree root system as it tunneled toward a house.

Considering those events that we missed, my timing was great. I picked one night in the high country that brought a typical storm. Only my fingers were numb. There were no snowdrifts or piles of ice. The tent stayed up. I remembered to take the stove inside before the rain started, and my children were stoic. All this was true—we had luck and grit. Still, this night will remain a mystery to me. I know it was worse than the records from nearby towns reflect. No one knows how fast the wind was hurtling into my tent as I braced my left arm against it. They don't have a weather station at 6,000 feet.

On this ridge, scientists could not measure a storm by what it knocked down: there were no buildings, no power lines, no mobile homes, and no large trees. There were just the ancient rhododendrons near clumps of pines, and our tent with me inside forming a human beam with my arms. Inside, I suffered the uprooting of my security. That can't be rebuilt.

THE DEAD HORSE

"Knowledge rests not upon truth alone, but upon error also."

—Carl Jung

I had failed to show Annie and Elizabeth the top of a mountain where only grass grew. We returned from Tennessee and slipped back into life at home with Nat, our friends, and obligations. The girls must go to school, and Nat and I must go to work. Routine filled the calendar. We cooked and ate and cleaned up, took baths, went to bed, attended church. Life was good—and full of stress. I longed to redeem myself after the disastrous overnight on one of the highest ridges in the Appalachians.

One year after that trip, I told Annie, now 7 years old, and Elizabeth, 9, that we would head back south, to Virginia this time. We could see their former babysitter, Bonnie, who had moved there. I called Bonnie and her husband, Karl, and they said they'd love to have us.

I longed for a few nights on the Appalachian Trail, using our bodies to feel the ground's rhythms, to lose the anxieties of regular life. I believed that if we could go back, walk through our discomforts, reach the tops of hills and cross muddy streams, the girls could experience that, as John Muir said, "going out . . . was really going in."

Bonnie drove us from her house in Bedford to a section of the Appalachian Trail that leads to the grassy fields of Grayson Highlands State Park. We'd see her at the end of the next day, when we would hike out to a different point on the AT.

We walked a few miles up a gentle rise through young woods that soon opened to a fringe of trees and a foggy meadow. We set up our tent in the grass near the Old Orchard Shelter, and I started the stove on the picnic table in front of the shelter. A dozen hikers were doing the same in and around the shelter. A light rain began, and we put on our raincoats and rain pants. The rain became steady, but still light, so I didn't worry. I told myself

After dinner with Annie (left) and Elizabeth, in raingear, at the Old Orchard Shelter. *Anonymous hiker*

I was handling things just fine. I had gotten the tent up by myself. I had fed my daughters. I had remembered the rain gear.

The next morning, I made hot cereal, and the girls packed their clothes as I dismantled the tent and stuffed it in my pack. We set off early in a chilly fog. I smiled at Annie's little yellow rainsuit and Elizabeth's matching set in blue. We hiked steadily uphill for a mile and a half. Near the top of Pine Mountain, they went ahead of me as the trail emerged out of the trees to a beautiful high meadow dotted with boulders. The sky was clearing, and the air warmed up. They took off their raincoats and rain pants. Annie raced to the top of one rock and raised her arms happily. She called down, "I have to run around, Mama! I'll see you later!" I smiled up at her and sighed with relief. She looked so happy. I hoped this was all turning out all right, but I was not sure the girls had slept soundly last night, and we were all a little tired from the long drive south before that. I checked my watch.

We put on our packs again and headed down a gravelly, narrow track that rolled down in gentle switchbacks through young trees with new leaves. Elizabeth's pack swung a little as she marched determinedly into this new valley. One hour went by, and we emerged at the bottom, in a large grassy area. We passed through a fence into a corral called the Scales. The sun was bright now. After stepping through the opening at the other fence, we unbuckled our pack straps and slid the heavy loads onto the sandy ground. We sat down, leaning against the wooden fenceposts. I pulled out three Ziploc bags of pepperoni, crackers, and cheese, and we munched our lunch, squinting in the sun.

A few minutes later, holding her lunch in her lap, Elizabeth fell asleep against the fencepost. We'd covered 3 miles and still had more than 5 miles left to walk to where Bonnie would pick us up. Elizabeth was only 9; she was carrying her own clothes, sleeping bag, and some of the food. Was I overdoing it? I opened my map of the Appalachian Trail through the Grayson Highlands. I should be very sure of where the AT continued out here. I frowned as I looked over at the next peak, Stone Mountain. A trail lay beyond the fence, but was it the continuation of the Appalachian Trail or not? I'd have to get up and scout a bit. In a minute.

Elizabeth slept on. Annie and I leaned back against the fence. I closed my eyes. A moment later I jolted awake to the sound of a pickup truck crunching on the gravel. It stopped near us. A ranger leaned his elbows on the steering wheel. I struggled up and ran over to the truck window. I smiled at him and opened my map. "Does that trail connect back to the Appalachian Trail?"

"There's a shorter way," he said. He opened his bigger map of Grayson Highlands State Park and pointed to a route. Then he gestured just beyond to a wide, level horse trail. It looked pleasant and not as steep as the AT. "That will save you time." He handed me his map. "Keep it."

"Hey, thanks!" I waved gaily as he drove away. I had a plan in my mind of where this shortcut would reconnect to the AT, so I didn't ask him to verify where the connection came. It seemed obvious to me.

We heaved on our packs and started trudging up the wide, hoof-chewed trail. It looked like a road, but the surface undulated, and we picked our way over loose sand and stones, between giant rhododendron bushes. I kept my head down, studying the hazards at my feet while chatting to encourage the girls.

"See these rhododendrons? Aren't they beautiful?" I called. "They're never this big in people's yards. I love the way they reach to the edge of the path." Soon the treadway met a stream that flowed not across the path, but straight down it through blotches of sun. Watching my steps in the water, I was not looking ahead, but suddenly smelled an odor of decay. A minute later, my boots reached a mass of blond hair flattened on the trail. I stopped. Then I saw teeth and an eye socket. My brain assembled the parts, and I realized that this was a dead horse.

Had some rider abandoned the animal? Then I remembered that wild ponies roam in the Grayson Highlands.

I had to break the news of this spectacle to the girls, who were still several yards back. I turned, wooden and smiling, and called out, "Uh—stay to the right, girls. Uh—there's a dead horse up here!"

We knew little of horses. Elizabeth and Annie had rarely been up close to one, and the days of horseback riding lessons lay deep in Annie's future. I had not brought them to the Grayson Highlands for the wild ponies specifically, although here roamed one of the few herds of semi-wild ponies in the East. The Grayson animals were descended from Virginia Highlander ponies released by Sugar Grove breeder William Pugh, who in the 1950s had begun experimenting with breeding smaller horses that could ramble strongly on mountains. Their grazing maintained the open land on abandoned farms that, in the mid-1960s, became the state park. Every spring a local association rounded up the ponies and sold a few at auction to keep the herd manageable.

They lived in the wild. And they died in the wild.

———————

The first time I encountered the largeness of a horse was a warm June Saturday in Princeton, New Jersey, at the Hospital Fete, the annual town fair put on by the local hospital. I was 4 or 5 years old, wearing a striped shirt that stretched across my still-round toddler tummy. My parents and I waited in line under the bright sun for what seemed like ages. The people in front of us would move a step forward, and then we would step forward. I could see trampled grass and a wire fence but could not see what was at the front of the line. Then we came to an opening in the temporary fence, where it widened into a circular corral. A lady in tan shorts lifted me high onto a brown pony. She told me to put my hand on the horn that stuck up off the saddle. I felt as if I would somersault over the horse's head. I didn't know this was Western riding, there in central New Jersey.

Such a quivery, slippery back. The leader guided the pony around a low wire fence set up for that day. With every thump of its legs, I tensed my body, first one side, then the other. I squinted in the sun's glare. Here and there around the circuit, the trampled grass had given way to dirt. We plodded by a line of tensely smiling adults as I concentrated on staying upright on the jolting, warm body. I could sense that this was an activity the grown-ups expected children to enjoy, and I was not at all sure I liked it, but I knew that it would not be kind to say so. I was waiting for the time I could get down. Ponies, which I thought were supposed babies based on books my parents and teachers had read to me, actually were gigantic. If it moved any faster, I'd slip right off. But the lady leading the animal was nice, and soon enough I came around the circuit to my mother and father. Immense relief.

Early in childhood—before you're aware that adults want you to show happiness, before you smile on cue for a camera—if you want to cry, you just cry, and if you want to laugh, you do so spontaneously. I was on the cusp between the baldly honest stage and the smile-on-cue stage. My parents must have felt that I would enjoy riding a horse, and I had not really enjoyed it. I was old enough not to cry but young enough that I could not pretend that I had liked it.

———————

I stood on the wide horse trail of Grayson Highlands State Park in the cool morning's mottled sun, mournfully considering the wild pony's carcass sprawled at my feet. I felt like a child again, awed by the size of a large, mysterious animal. I saw no way around it; we must step over the remains. To me its face looked pained, even though I knew it obviously now felt nothing.

The girls caught up and saw the body. I tried to explain, "It's natural to die. It's even normal for a horse like this to stay where it died."

I had brought them to a place where a horse could fall over dead and no one cared.

Other parents have told me their children mouth off when they're upset or at least tell them what's on their minds. My children have always become really quiet. They were silent now.

We stepped over it, and I stopped talking. The stream we had sloshed through now turned away from the path, which soon after forked. The ranger had said nothing about a fork. I sighed and paused and then realized the girls were watching me hesitate. I must choose. So I turned us left as the most logical route. We hiked out over a treeless area with a view of Mount Rogers, the highest point in Virginia. Glorious sun lit up meadows stretching to distant ridges. The girls' hair blew in the wind and they held plastic bags of M&Ms. They looked carefree. But I was not. I was rethinking our location. We should not have come this far without meeting up with the Appalachian Trail. I said nothing but sank to my knees with the ranger's map and placed my own map next to it. *Oh.* The left fork had added 3 miles to our afternoon's route. It looked now as if we still had at least 5 miles to go, and it was getting late. The ranger must have thought we were headed in the other direction on the AT. I hadn't actually told him our destination, Massie Gap.

The girls were watching me studying the map too long. So I said, "OK, the good news is that I know where we are! We have to keep going for a while longer."

Annie and Elizabeth near Mount Rogers, Viriginia.

They said nothing. We slogged on, hardly speaking for the next hour and a half. I was beginning to deflate, and so I reached deep for some bit of cheer. "We're getting there," I panted. *Why aren't we getting there?* I asked myself. Did Elizabeth and Annie realize I was barely holding on?

We crossed a fast-moving stream that would have been lovely had I not been dazed with worry. I heard a rustling sound and then saw two men walking toward us, hiking with large packs. We stopped, and they stopped, and I asked, "Do you know how far it is to the parking lot?"

"Where are you headed?"

"Massie Gap," I said, noticing that my voice quavered.

They frowned. It looked as if they were trying to measure my capabilities by how I looked standing with my hands on my wind pants. Then they nodded at me. I could tell that they had decided not to ask why I did not know how far I had to go. That is, they were letting me save face in front of my children. I wanted to hug them.

"Go up over that ridge," one of them said in a businesslike tone, handing me his water bottle, which I took and immediately poured into my empty one. He pointed to a ridge of bushes and granite. "Massie Gap is that way, but you have to go over that mountain first. It's about a mile." I realized it would be another mile beyond that.

I thanked the men and then with my best late-day field voice, I said, "OK, girls, it's just a mile over the ridge, and then it's all downhill!"

They seemed relieved and lighthearted after that. The last mountain emerged and retreated quickly as we marched. Elizabeth started jogging down the final slope just ahead of me. She tripped and landed shoulder-first in the dusty dirt. She wailed and sat up, a gash on her arm seeping red. I knelt down, retrieved the first-aid sack, and bandaged the cut. We were truly almost there.

Much later that night, tucked into beds at Bonnie's house, the girls lay awake. I puttered around pulling out pajamas and my toothbrush.

"Mama?" Annie asked.

"Yes, Annie?"

"I'm afraid of the horse."

"Oh." I paused. "Annie." I listened to her quiet breathing. "Try to put it out of your mind." (I was afraid of the horse, too, but did not say that.)

Silence. "Try thinking of something else." This was not a good response, but my voice felt gentler than my racing mind.

From the other bed, Elizabeth said quietly, "Think about cupcakes."

The brave voice of optimism. I loved it. I had been scared, too, but not of the horse. I had feared getting lost, running out of water, being injured. As their mother, my obligation lay in putting those fears aside. We were all safe now. We had helped each other through. Elizabeth's optimism soothed me. But I had taken them the wrong way. The dead horse was my fault. It was not a random thing. We had found the horse because of my mistake. And yet I hoped that the horse could not scare us again.

ABANDONED TRUCK

Backpacks strapped on, Elizabeth, Annie, and I stood roadside in Catawba, Virginia, waiting for a break in the rushing lines of cars and trucks. We looked right, then left, then right. Sun flashed off windshields. A gap in the traffic opened up and we skittered across the sharp curve of Route 311. The bright sun could not warm the air's chill. On the other side we stepped into the trees, onto the Appalachian Trail, to start the gentle switchback up the side of McAfee Knob.

An hour later, we arrived panting on the granite cliff that stuck out like a giant tongue over the pastures and meadows of Roanoke County. The knob is one of the most popular retreats near Roanoke, south of the Shenandoah Valley. But on this April weekday of year three in the all-girl trips, we had the cliff to ourselves. Green velvet fields, tin roofs, red buildings, and rolled hay bales all fell away underneath light-blue sky. The fields looked near, but we were just high enough that we could not see any people in the valley. We took turns posing and taking pictures of each other on the cliff.

On the cliff of McAfee Knob near Roanoke, Virginia. *Annie Spencer-Eddy Levine*

Chiseled onto a flat area of rock was *R. S. Kime, 1909*. Sachem Kime had grown up climbing the mountain but left the area to serve in World War I. He returned as an adult, and one day when he was in his 30s, sitting in a barbershop in Salem, he looked up at the knob and announced he would like to own it. A man standing in the shop said *he* owned the land. "It's undeveloped, and it never has been surveyed. If you can get a survey, I'd be willing to trade it," the man reportedly told Kime. So Kime did that and received a deed for a triangular plot around the knob. Many years later, the National Park Service asked him if he would sell it to protect the Appalachian Trail. Kime offered to donate it instead.

But others who owned land near the knob weren't so generous. A former U.S. Navy doctor named Harry Johnson owned a tract that spanned the area near McAfee Knob to halfway down nearby Catawba Mountain. He had built a beautiful lodge as a retreat and hoped to build a house right on the knob. Johnson once told Mike Dawson, a regional representative for the Appalachian Trail Conference, that the whole trail project "was an enormous boondoggle and outside the U.S. Constitution." For eight years, the federal government negotiated with Johnson, whose lodge sat unused except when the curious barged in and vandalized it. He eventually sold his land to the Park Service.

Houses, cabins, and Johnson's old lodge all had been torn down by the time the girls and I climbed the ridge. Wilderness had crept in on top of former houses. One family still lived on the other side of the ridge, but eventually that house, too, would go .

Johnson's drawn-out protest signaled the era of the government actively taking land for the AT. In the trail's early years, between the 1930s and 1960s, property owners along the route had simply let walkers go through. But in 1968, the federal government passed the National Trail Systems Act and began systematically working to acquire land around the AT route. Officials condemned some of it, bought some of it, and negotiated land protection on some of it.

———

Beyond the knob, Elizabeth, Annie, and I walked between ancient rhododendrons, descended a few hundred feet, and came to a place where, not many years before, a man named Sherril Smith had lived directly underneath the electric power lines. He kept a half-dozen pigs that would run at random under the wires and follow the Appalachian Trail land stewards as they did surveying work. Now this area was called Pig Farm Campsite. But Smith had not really farmed. Most of the pastures we had admired below the knob true were not true working farms, either. We would not camp on the old pig run, pretty though this ridge was. I had learned not to pitch a tent on an open ridge.

We continued two more miles to Lamberts Meadow Shelter. The trees here were young, no more than 8 inches in diameter, because of the high winds and thin soil. The fringe of vegetation did block some of the wind around the three-sided structure. But I told the girls, "We'll set up our tent, just in case other hikers come. We can have our privacy." Plus we'd be out of that wind, which felt cold. I gave Elizabeth the task of finding a level spot

Annie descends a stile.

on the southeast side of the shelter, where it was less windy. She chose the spot, and I set up the tent. I realized I would be sleeping on a medium-sized tree root, but I didn't move the tent, out of respect for Elizabeth's choice.

"I'm going for water," I said. "Anyone want to come?" Annie leaped up: "I do." Elizabeth said she'd rest in the tent. We strolled a quarter-mile across the meadow, under power lines and down an old road to the spring. A pipe channeled it along the ground for 20 feet until it poured into a runoff stream. It was flowing strong, gurgling into pools of water. I leaned down to the largest pool and scooped potfuls of water into the open cap of my old nylon water bag.

When we returned to the tent, Annie told Elizabeth about the pipe and the pools, and Elizabeth wanted to go back with us after we ate our pasta. I needed to collect more water for our early breakfast. The sun was dipping low, and, as I asked, the girls paddled their hands downstream of where I was gathering water. They carried their stuffed animals along the edges of the water flow. I half listened to their soft voices making up stories about their animals. They lay their bandannas on the gravel, letting the water clean them. They leaped over mudholes and up and down the stream banks. How much joy and imagination they found in a piped spring!

Standing 20 yards back so I would not interfere with their play, I saw at a faint roadbed leading downhill. The grass-covered route ran parallel to a stone foundation. I ambled over to look at the wall, wondering what other remnants of former habitation I might find. I did not ask the girls to come. It was almost dusk now, and I didn't want them to feel afraid as the dark settled in. I put my hand on my headlamp in my pocket, reassuring myself. Then I noticed something in the distance: the hulk of an old truck.

I walked downslope to it. The side had the faded words *Valleydale Meats*, but the *V* had mostly worn off. The rusted back doors sat partway open, so I peered inside. I could see little in the gloom except that the bottom of the truck slanted at an unnatural angle, and it had giant rust-edged holes. I could make out a bent metal framework.

An animal could take refuge in there, or someone might duck inside to escape a storm. I tried to imagine this truck back when it worked, back when someone drove up the mountain on this old road now covered by grass and saplings.

I realized I was neglecting Elizabeth and Annie. I turned away from the truck and returned quickly to the stream. They were still dragging their bandannas through the water and running up and down. "Let's go back to the tent, girls." Brisk. Confident.

I had read people were seeing mountain lions (also called cougars, catamounts, panthers, and ghost cats) in this area. I said nothing to the girls about it, but all day I had been glancing around as we walked. Could big cats be skulking up here? The U.S. Fish and Wildlife Service had declared mountain lions extinct east of the Rocky Mountains. The animals had once thrived in every state east of the Mississippi River, but scientists believe they have been gone from the East since about World War II, except for the small subspecies known as the Florida panther. Ghost cats persist in the community imagination, in the culture, and some say in truth. Since 1970, 121 sightings have been reported in Virginia. But most likely the big cats disappeared sometime in the 1800s, coinciding with the near-disappearance of the white-tailed deer over hundreds of years of tree cutting and hunting. In 2018, years after this trip, the federal government removed the eastern mountain lion from the endangered species list on the grounds that one cannot protect what does not exist.

We walked several paces away from the tent with our toothbrushes. I poured a little water in the girls' cups. We brushed our teeth and spit into the thick leaf cover. I pushed dead leaves over where we'd spit. Back in our nylon home, we burrowed into our sleeping bags. "You did so well today," I remember telling them before saying a slightly rambling prayer, thanking God for the mountain, for our time, praying for Nat and our cat Smudgie, and of course the long list of relatives on both sides of the family, starting with the grandmothers. Then I kissed both girls good night.

A few minutes later, I unzipped the door and headed back outside to look around for movement: raccoons, porcupines, bears...mountain lions?

It was too early for leaves on the trees, so I could see lights in the distance: many, many white lights all arranged in neat grids far down, way beyond where I stood, but so near they seemed to speak. The city of Roanoke. I had forgotten about it. There would be no mountain lions tonight.

CAMOUFLAGE

I was haunted by the night on Grassy Ridge, huddled inside a fabric tent with Elizabeth and Annie while the driving rain and thunder howled around us. The terror of lightning. The weight of responsibility. Going into year four of the great all-girl spring vacation backpacking experiment, I still clutched that memory of fear above 6,000 feet close to my heart, part of my Gore-Tex rain gear–clad soul.

I avoided leading Elizabeth and Annie *knowingly* into bad weather. If the forecast were for hard rain or snow or something else ugly, we would wait to go. The problem was that the Southern Appalachians vibrate with storms in April. For the past two April vacations we had hiked at slightly lower elevations.

Something in me still argued with my decision to go or not go based on the weather. My big goal in taking the girls backpacking every spring was to show that when you're backpacking, you take what comes. You might gallop through sun-washed meadows, but you also might splash through soaking thigh-high grasses that make you set your jaw and slog on. But that's when you get the benefits. You see (I might say to them), the real joy, the real triumph comes after, when your proud mother hugs you and says, "You did it. You got through something hard. Those boys on the playground cannot hurt your pride, ever, when you've fought through that kind of thing." The girls, of course, might have responded that they weren't telling the boys about their backpacking. They weren't talking a lot about it at all. Annie told me once that she had realized that most families went to Disney but ours went camping. I laughed with pride at the time, but I frowned with doubt later. We were weird. I was weird.

Now, year four, April vacation, and I'd packed us up for the annual all-girl camping trip in southwestern Virginia, along the Appalachian Trail. We would stage the final departure from Bonnie and Karl's house in Bedford, Virginia. The girls loved visiting them, and so did I.

Bonnie had always cared for us like family. Now she stepped in as chief weather watcher and insisted that we wait a few days for a dry forecast. I could not argue, and if I had asked her to drive us in the rain, that conversation might have gone on for a while with the same result: wait until Bonnie felt ready to take us. She had always been a mother figure to me. In the years she watched the girls a few hours a day, I had taken her ideas to heart. When she would tell me I looked tired or that I was trying to do too many things, she was always right.

So. Muddy ditches. Good weather or bad weather. Life is not a Hallmark movie, but I knew that Bonnie had a point. Why set us up for an endurance march and maybe some wailing? Our backpacks stuffed with gear and food, we waited an extra two nights.

Bonnie put us in a very comfortable guest room on the basement level. I had my own bed, and each girl had her own bed in the enormous room. A little kitchenette sat at one end with a coffee maker and snacks. I sighed with happiness when we went down there for bedtime. I appreciated my solitude after the girls started dozing off.

In the middle of the night, I reached down to the floor to steady myself as I got out of bed. I felt water. *Hmm.* I put my socked feet down on the floor. *Squish.* My notebook and books I'd put on the floor were soaked like floppy sponges. I put all my stuff up high, visited the bathroom, changed my socks, and got through to the morning. To me, this was nothing: all my years in the woods had shown me far worse discomfort. Upstairs, I said good morning and announced that we had a little water on the floor. Bonnie was horrified.

I failed to see the meaning of this indoor flood occurring as we waited for good weather. Now, of course, the lesson comes through. We slept in there waiting for safety, but we can never truly protect ourselves.

Bad things can bring good things, I wrote in my diary while dozing off on a sofa bed in the upstairs living room the next night.

I made two lists. Bad thing: A flood in Bonnie's basement soaked this journal. Good thing: They might not have known their basement was flooded without our being down there that night. Bad thing: We had to wait an extra two days to get onto the trail. Good thing: We went to the local library and I had time to reread T. S. Eliot's *The Four Quartets*, the singular piece of literature the Eight Legs had taken on the Appalachian Trail.

We spent hours in the library that day, reading with no pressures on us. Breathless, I veered into Eliot's fourth quartet, "Little Gidding," and read about the unsettled time of early spring, which he called "midwinter spring." We were deep in that season that week.

Two days later, finally, the rain was letting up. Karl dropped us off at the trailhead on Route 60. We waved as he pulled away, hoisted on our packs, and then hiked past a recently burned section of forest. A light rain began. "Let's just keep going through it, girls," I said. "It's not bad."

We descended out of the burned section into a young forest. The rain stopped after about an hour. We came up to a man and a boy standing on the side of the trail. "We were waiting out the rain under the trees," the man said. "Where are you headed?" I said Cow Camp Gap. He said they were going there too.

"You hiked through the rain?" he asked. I said yes. He and the boy, who looked about 9 or 10, both wore camouflage jackets. I found their clothing a little unsettling. It meant to me that they were primarily hunters. I did not know many hunters. Morally the practice does not offend me, but I feel very different from them. Hunters train themselves to observe and wait, while backpackers feel the need to move forward. They had probably huddled in the trees during the rain. I thought, but did not say, that such strategies can prevent making headway.

"My wife and daughter, his sister, dropped us off," he said, adding that the females in his family weren't interested in camping. I smiled. They set off just ahead of us, and I led the girls a little more slowly to keep distance as we all hiked toward the shelter turnoff.

The shelter was small, and a few other hikers had spread out their stuff in it. I chose a flat area just beyond the picnic table for our tent. I handed Elizabeth and Annie the ends of the long pole pieces while I snapped them into place. They positioned themselves at one end, each holding the pole and the fabric pocket it now rested in while I maneuvered the other end into its own pocket.

"Want a hand with that?" the dad asked me.

"I've got it," I said. The fabric dome wobbled into place.

At some point in his chatter, I wondered if I should feel nervous. Was he a little too interested in us? Maybe this man did not have our best interests at heart. So I watched him and the boy for a while. The father was doing a lot of things I was doing: getting up the tent, pulling out food, setting up his stove, talking to his child.

He had his son with him, after all. He was as devoted, I could see, to helping that boy learn self-reliance as I was to teaching my girls the same lesson. We were on parallel teams with matching agendas. But he was a stranger whose default had been not to believe that I could be doing all this. I did not ask him for one bit of help.

"I'm going to tell my wife about you," he said as we all cooked our dinners on the picnic table. "I've never seen girls out like this. Could I take your picture to show her?"

"Sure," I said. "Come on, girls." They clustered on either side of me as I sat on the picnic table.

He positioned his camera. "She will not believe it."

At least three other campers were clattering around, setting up in the shelter and sharing the picnic table. In many ways this resembled a typical night on the Appalachian Trail. But my own understanding was evolving,

Elizabeth (left), Annie (right) and I eat breakfast at Cow Camp Gap Shelter. *Anonymous hiker dad*

as if I'd pulled back a movie camera on the scene and could imagine, for a second, why Nat might worry about us when we went out as the all-girl team. I also could see myself: a capable, aware, skilled, caring mother. We weren't doing this perfectly by any means. But we were doing it.

Elizabeth and Annie and I shared a quiet laugh in our tent later. Those guys had asked if we needed help! This scene echoed Elizabeth's playground encounter with the boy who had told her girls weren't strong. The father and son had witnessed that the opposite was true. I put aside my discomfort. I had judged them, as they had judged us. I thought I understood their attitudes because they wore camouflage.

911

Packing and leaving for a camping trip the April that Elizabeth was 12 and Annie 10 comprised the greatest feat of multitasking I'd ever performed. Work, school, and the busiest religious week of our year, Holy Week and Easter. A late night at the Maundy Thursday vigil after singing in the choir. Services and baking on Good Friday. Choir rehearsal on Saturday, Easter services and family reunions on Sunday. The youth group had an overnight. Which meant everyone in our household was down on sleep.

Sometime during all this, my brother John, who worked as a weather observer at Newark International Airport, called. He had been looking at the forecasts for North Carolina and Tennessee.

"Johnny, is it going to rain much?"

"Well, no," he said. "It's going to be *cold*."

"Oh, the mountains are always a little cold," I replied. He did not say much more, just quoted some temperatures from cities nearest to our destination. I cannot remember the numbers. I ignored them to preserve my resolve. I already knew I was headed to a part of the Tennessee mountains that sits buried under far worse weather than surrounding areas, even though there was no hard proof of that because it is so remote, despite access by a state road. No buildings, no thermometers, no weather stations. No forecasts. I still hoped that what had happened before in that place would not happen again. I yearned to take Elizabeth and Annie to Grassy Ridge. We had stopped way short of it in 1997, that night in the thunderstorm.

The night before Easter, I was totally exhausted from staying up late Thursday, preparing Easter baskets, and baking hot cross buns and side dishes, but I dragged out all the camping gear. I measured pancake mix into Ziploc bags with the phone cradled on my left shoulder, talking to my sister-in-law about Easter dinner.

I threw the empty backpacks and everything I would stuff in them— stove, fuel, first-aid kit, and sacks of food—into the station wagon. Nat, the girls, and I drove to White Plains, New York, after church for a walk and a family dinner. Right after dinner, I kissed Nat and everyone else goodbye, and the girls and I pulled away on the first leg of our long drive south. The first night, we'd stay with Nat's sister in Allentown, Pennsylvania; the second night, in a motel somewhere farther along the 800-mile route; finally, day three, Tuesday, we would start hiking in to Grassy Ridge, the place we had left in 1997 after that overnight storm.

I had found everything we needed except one item: the Swiss Army knife, the camping multitool that would open cans, cut ropes and gauze, and maybe even protect us in a pinch. There was no way I could open the can of tomato paste I'd brought for the first night on the trail without something like that knife. I made a note to buy one on the road. I was sure we would pass a suitable store sometime in the next two days.

Another problem was dogging me. My brother's words about the weather forecast.

Early Monday morning I steered our 1987 Chevrolet Celebrity station wagon onto the Pennsylvania Turnpike and started listening to weather reports as I drove. We stopped that night at a motel off Interstate 81 in southern Virginia. The television weatherman gestured violently at his map. A swirl of cold air and snow was going to hover tomorrow night over a giant swath of the East. The southern end of that blob seemed to hit at about the spot where we would be camping after a 3-mile hike.

I knew that taking the girls down there in April again was risky. I knew that if I believed that Grassy Ridge's weather lies outside of weather stations, the weather there might be *worse* than the forecast: colder, windier, wetter. Yet I hoped for warmer, manageable, dry enough. Hadn't we seen already the worst conditions that ridge could throw at us? It could not get uglier than 1997's all-night thunderstorm. At least, that was what I told myself.

———————

On Tuesday afternoon, we arrived in the town of Roan Mountain, Tennessee. I hoped to find a store before we drove the last 14 miles up to the trailhead. I had to buy a small camp knife or multitool of some sort or we weren't going to have sauce on our spaghetti. The radio announcer had just said it was 40 degrees out. Occasional little bursts of snow flurries veered into the windshield. I stopped the station wagon outside a small general store, and we all went in. I scanned the small aisles. "Do you have pen knives or can openers?" I asked. The clerk shook her head. "No."

We walked over to a pharmacy. "Someone else asked me for a pen knife," the clerk said. "Maybe I ought to stock them."

I wandered up and down the aisles anyway. Maybe a forgotten can opener was hanging somewhere. I fixed on a shiny object encased in plastic: momentary hope, then disappointment. Eyelash curlers. I had seen those hanging in the general store, too. The eyelash curlers resembled small crowbars. I had never even picked up these contraptions, let alone squeezed them on my eyelash hairs. *How* could I have left home without that pen knife?

How ironic, I thought, that the last town before the Appalachian Trail crossing sold beauty products but nothing that would open a can of soup. I must be the only mother on the continent who takes her daughters camping. I wanted my girls to get used to being away from things, to get good at basic survival skills, like cooking outside. I thought this would move them into another kind of reality, that zone of the mountains in which you forget about civilized life and start loving simple things. Where you leave behind the world of appearances, including curled eyelashes.

The road to Carvers Gap in snow. *Mitch West*

In the intervening years since we'd last been to this area, the girls and I had hiked at slightly lower elevations in Virginia. Now we were back at higher elevation, and winter had not moved out yet. *By God*, I thought, sniffing in the cold breeze as we left the pharmacy, *let's go*. We were so close. We were going to drive up that road out of this little town and we were going to hike up to Grassy Ridge, because I had promised Elizabeth and Annie I would show them mountains with grass on top.

We climbed back into the car, and I decided I would improvise with the extra food. No can opening. We were out of prep time.

I steered the Chevy out of town onto Route 19E. Sunshine played with clouds and alternated with flurries. Snowflakes now coated the road signs. We had 14 miles to go up to the trail crossing. Grassy fields dotted with houses and churches passed by our windows. We drove by the Lighthouse for Christ Church, the White Head Hill Bible Christian Church, the Little Mountain Baptist Church, and the Open Bible Hour Ministries. I turned onto Route 143, and we entered Roan Mountain State Park. We roared past the Sugar Hollow Freewill Baptist Church and the Burbank Freewill Baptist Church and crossed into Cherokee National Forest.

Farther up the ridge, the road switchbacked around a mountain, as roads do to avoid going straight up. Our tires rolled over thin layers of snow on the northern patches of road. Then we would veer around on the southern side of the switchback and roll onto clear pavement again. After two or three times of this, we rounded a bend toward the north, and suddenly the snow covered the asphalt entirely and was falling more heavily than it had been just a moment ago at slightly lower elevation. And it was getting thicker by the second. Nothing had been plowed yet. I had to steer the Chevy into a single set of tire tracks—really just depressions—up the road's center.

The tracks made little ridges of snow on either side. *Just keep going*, I thought. On our right, the land fell sharply away beyond the short guardrail. I didn't like this. I wondered what it would be like when we came back down two days from now.

Suddenly, I was panicking. I shifted the car into the lowest gear. Annie called from the back: "Mem? Mem? Mem?" (Her nickname for me.)

"Annie, don't talk to me just now! I'm trying to drive!" I kind of yelled. Dead silence in the back. And just as quickly as my temper flared, I realized that I was defeated. This was not working. So I did the thing that no one who lives in New England ever does in the snow.

I stopped the car.

Now only the sound of my frustrated breathing, in and out, in and out, could be heard in the car. My brain was noisy, though. I was shouting inside: *I am not driving any farther, either up or down! I am not!* I forgot all about pen knives, gear, plans, the rest of it. I went into a kind of low-grade survival mode, focused more on disappointment than true fears for our safety. We were in here, and warm, and we hadn't fallen off the mountain. We had driven 800 miles only to stop the car in a spring snowstorm. My peripheral vision caught my sweet little girls quietly sitting in the back. What total angels. I did not deserve their patience. God bless them for not hassling me! We sat there for a minute.

I remembered that I had an early model cell phone in the car, which I hadn't used in two years; it had been an experiment at work that we'd abandoned, a nearly useless piece of plastic and metal. People were starting to carry better cell phones, but I had so far resisted getting another one. But maybe this relic could help. I rummaged in the glove compartment and grabbed the giant gray phone and its cord, plugging it into the cigarette lighter. "I'm going to call 911," I said, trying to sound casual. But my heart started to race, and my hands shook as I brought them up to my face. "I'm sorry, girls!" I sobbed.

"Mem, it's OK! You didn't know!" they said. I wondered if they were right. Or terrified. As usual, they didn't go into detail about their inner thoughts. I was taking up all the emotional space with my own feelings.

The phone worked. I dialed 911 and heard static. The phone display glowed the message: "Send to redial." This was what cell phones did back then. The reception was so terrible that most of the time the connections didn't go through, or if they did, they lasted only a few seconds. I dialed again. More static. After a third and fourth time, I finally heard a click and a ring and then the serious monotone voice of a dispatcher. I could not make out what she said. Maybe the name of the district. What should I say? I talked to dispatchers twice a week at my job at home, but that was as a reporter. I'd never been the needy party.

"Hi," I said. "We're stuck on the road into Carver's Gap. There's 6 inches of snow, I'm afraid to keep going, and I can't turn the car around." My voice quavered. "I'm here with my two children."

The woman asked, "What county are you in?"

What *county*? She was asking me something I could not answer. I felt the old anger well up again.

"I don't know what county," I snapped. "Um, I'm almost at Carver's Gap. I was in the town of Roan Mountain."

"Do you think you're in *Carter* County?" she asked.

That sounded vaguely familiar from one of my maps, which I hadn't thought to consult before calling. "I think so."

She asked my name, where we were from, who was with me, what kind of car we drove. The car: a 1987 Chevy Celebrity that someone in our church had given us that had fake wood on the sides. It used to be navy blue and now was a kind of faded grayish color, and the edges where the wood affixed had loose bits of what looked like old tape. I laughed at our car sometimes, but the truth was that it was a very solid machine that had gotten us across the country and back the previous summer. I was sorry that I wasn't giving it a chance to show what it could do on a snowy mountain.

So we waited for emergency help.

I didn't want to cry now. As we sat there, I realized that I felt good that we had at least *tried* to drive to our camping trip's beginning point, despite the cold weather forecast. The night before, as we watched the weather report on TV, Annie, perched on the edge of the motel bed, had told me with her usual intensity that she wanted to go. I could not disappoint this determined, serious child when we were still at the motel, so I reasoned that the weather report covered valley conditions, even though I knew by now that weather in the valley has very little to do with the mountain (and usually the mountain is worse).

As we sat there waiting for rescue, I saw a pickup truck coming down the mountain toward us. I began to open the window to gesture. A spray of snow landed on the car as the truck whirred by and away. He wasn't calling 911.

"Well, girls, would you like some lunch?" I asked. My heart was beating more normally now that the professionals were on the way. I struggled into my down coat and gloves, hopped out of the car, and opened up the back hatch for the lunch bag. I passed it through. The girls started unwrapping cheese slices and pulling out crackers, and I actually thought to step outside and take a picture of our stranded car. I felt a little stupid doing this, but I thought it might be an important moment that should be recorded.

I was back in the Chevy when another car approached. I looked in the rearview mirror and could see a small SUV behind us. It slowed, and I opened my window. The SUV pulled alongside our car. Two men who looked to be in their early 20s, both with longish hair and new beards, peered out, looking concerned. The one nearer to me asked, "Are you all right?"

"No," I said.

I got out then to explain our predicament. We actually were all right. It was our ability to go farther that was not all right. One of them said, "Well, you could turn the car around and get down the mountain."

"You don't realize," I told them, "I'm not in the right state of mind to turn the car around. Would you do it? Would you drive my car back down the mountain?"

"We could turn the car around for you," the sandy-haired man at the wheel said. He got out and I walked around to the passenger side and watched as he sat in the driver's seat and adjusted the seat. He did an expert K-turn and within minutes had the Chevy wagon pointed downhill.

I asked again, "But could you also drive it back down the mountain for me? I'm afraid to do that."

The two men looked something between incredulous and amused.

I kept thinking of the thick snow, the barely discernable, slippery tracks, and the low guardrail and steep dropoff.

So I asked a few more times.

I do not know why I trusted these two men. Perhaps it was that the two alternatives to letting them drive my car down seemed worse. The sheriff might arrest me for driving in bad conditions after coming to rescue us; at the least, my daughters and I would be sitting in a police station for hours. The other option, driving that car myself down the snowy switchbacks, made me panic. I did not want to terrify Elizabeth and Annie as well. I'd already done enough, taking them to a place with its own microclimate, where winter still raged at nearly 6,000 feet, for the second time in three years near Grassy Ridge. Why would their mother insist on torturing them here? Did the place feel hexed?

The two young men had offered help, and I was taking the risk of asking for even more help.

The driver said yes. He would take us down, and the other man would follow in their car. "Great!" I said. I picked up the dinosaur phone and called the 911 dispatcher back. "Hi, this is the lady who called before," I said. "I'm stuck on the road into Carver's Gap. Two guys have come along to help me. They have turned my car around, and one of them is going to drive it down the mountain for me."

"OK," she said. "If he wants to take on that liability, that risk. If he wants to do that, that's up to him." I held the phone away and stuck my body halfway out of my turned-around car and called, "She wants me to ask if you are sure you want to do this." I didn't use the words *risk* or *liability*.

"Yeah," the driver said.

"He's going to do it," I said.

She repeated, "If he wants to take that risk, that liability, I just wanted you to know that we would not do that. We were sending the sheriff up there. He would not have driven your car. He would take you somewhere and you would call a wrecker."

The drama these men were helping us escape began to unfold in my mind. I pictured the girls and me sitting in the state park's deserted visitors' center, wrapped in our sleeping bags for three hours, while I tried to reach AAA. I imagined the sheriff making out a report about me, issuing a ticket, maybe, for third-degree reckless endangerment or first-degree stupidity by a mother who drove her young daughters up the ridge in this sort of weather.

"I really appreciate your calling back," the dispatcher said.

"Thank you for your help."

I felt relieved now, even happy. Maybe I ought to have felt embarrassed, but my whole self radiated joy.

I don't know why I thought I couldn't turn my car around. They had done it so easily. But I had panicked and felt imprisoned. Two young girls were depending on me. Now I turned to my journalistic instincts: I asked our driver about himself. His name was Scott R——. I asked if he would write his name in my spiral notebook, and he carefully printed it out. He lived in Johnson City, the last settlement of any real size before the mountains. (*That* town would have sold Swiss Army knives.) Scott said, "We're going to drive back up to the gap and then walk into a makeshift campsite we used last week in a storm." I wondered if I were too wimpy. Then I changed my mind. I was not. *We* were not.

This lesson about weather hit me strong as a tempest. I knew I would never forget that what the calendar calls spring, the mountains call winter. Let the April winds howl without us. We could go back to find those grass-topped mountains—in late May. Or June.

But after Scott drove the car out of the storm, and my panic receded, I wished just a little that the girls and I could stick around and get this trip right. We could return to the mountain two days later, when soft spring air and sun would again hover over Tennessee.

But home responsibilities beckoned. Elizabeth and Annie had to go back to school in a few days. I drove to Laurel Fork Gorge, and we took a short hike. I put down my camera during a rest and had to run back for it. I felt a little addled; I'd just called 911 an hour earlier, after all. The snow at the gorge had just dusted the mountain laurels. The waterfall crashed down in the gray, cold afternoon.

Later we began the long drive home, stopping on the way to see two friends who had moved to South Carolina—a lovely visit. We were almost too clean, too well cared for. Joy is diminished without hardship.

Life is storms. Life is weather. And it's one of few things people can't control. Was this the lesson I had actually sought for Elizabeth and Annie? Stepping over to the other side, to the unpredictability of the elements, setting up another doomed camping trip? Was *that* it? Was it the disasters that drew the girls and me closer and helped us became stronger and more self-reliant because things went wrong?

This time I could not get us to the wilds. The tempests had pushed us back. I put my energy into transforming disappointment and my flirtation with true fear into the fact that we had come through it without tears or anxiety. Something will always go wrong. My work as the all-girl hike leader was not yet done here.

OVERMOUNTAIN

July 9, 2002: Elizabeth, Annie, and I stepped onto the open meadow and the Appalachian Trail at Carver's Gap. For the third time in six years, we were setting out for Grassy Ridge, to see mountains where only grass grows on top. I'd finally yielded to April weather's instability and moved the trip to summer. I hoped that this reconnaissance with the southern balds would quiet a restlessness in me. I had built up this quest to reach Grassy Ridge as a kind of pilgrimage to Shangri-la, a place beautifully removed from the civilized world. I'd been promising the girls since they were toddlers that I would show them one of my favorite places in the mountains.

That first year, we'd started out of Carver's Gap in late afternoon under dark clouds. Then we'd endured the violent storm, awakened soaking wet, and retreated before we could hike to Grassy Ridge. The second try, four years later, I'd had to call for help while we were still in the car; we'd marshalled two young men to help us turn around in the snow.

Elizabeth, 13, carries more of the food and gear.

This time I pulled into the little gravel parking lot at Carver's Gap in midmorning. Sun bathed the meadows on either side. We heaved our packs on our backs, I locked the car, and we started up Round Bald. The last time we had seen it was in fog. Today, the thick grasses were a rich green reaching away in all directions. We continued over Jane Bald and Grassy Ridge Bald. When we were steps away from the summit of Grassy Ridge Bald, I turned around and faced Elizabeth and Annie as they hiked toward me. The wind was rippling the tall grasses. I put my hands out and smiled.

I said nothing. I did not have to. They nodded.

Standing there with the bright-green meadow waving around, I felt part of that ridge as if I were speaking a new language of connection—no language that has ever existed before but which guides me into respect for the natural cycles around us. David Abram, the ecologist, wrote, "Whenever I quiet the persistent chatter of words within my head, I find this silent or wordless dance always already going on this improvised duet between my animal body and the fluid, breathing landscape that it inhabits."

I eventually learned that my daughters had come without complaint to this region three times because they could see how deep my yearnings were. They told me years later that they felt sad those times we hadn't reached the

Annie, 11, hikes toward Grassy Ridge.

places I so wanted to go. They didn't want me to be disappointed. Was I showing them those places where the mind, soul, and wilderness join together? Where a girl learns courage? Yes, perhaps. Were they teaching me patience and perseverance through their own kindness, because they rarely complained? Definitely.

We walked the next few miles to an old barn known as the Overmountain Shelter, also called Yellow Mountain Barn. Back in 1997, that first trip, I had planned for us to spend two days getting to this barn, because the girls were so little. As we hiked over the ridge now, past the turnoff for the 1997 campsite, I thought of how beautiful that exposed meadow location had been. But I didn't want to go back there. The thunderstorm and sleepless night replayed in my mind every so often, and since that experience on Grassy Ridge, all three of us now quaked every time we heard thunder.

The skies remained clear. We made it past all the landmarks of the first year, across Grassy Ridge, and reached shelter before dusk. After dinner, we lay inside our sleeping bags on our mats in the barn's loft. It could rain now, and we would not feel a drop. A wide-open door at one end let in the dissipating light. An owl hooted.

Although I wanted to feel totally secure, I felt a little uneasy, as I always did when I was the only adult. But even that wariness, six years into the all-girl project, felt comfortable now. I had adapted to worrying. I'd learned that I could handle driving rain, fog, and bad weather and do it while motivating two young girls to keep moving. And they were older now—13 and 11—and taller, with more strength and a mental resilience about camping that I admired.

Elizabeth and Annie lay quietly in their sleeping bags. Maybe they were asleep already. I sprawled on my stomach, scrawling notes in red ink in a tiny notebook. I kept thinking I heard the crunch of an animal on the gravelly path outside or a mouse skittering near us on the floor. I would pop my head up, turn toward sound that I likely just imagined. After all, my hearing is pretty terrible.

We climbed the next day over the rippling grasses of the Humps, more stunning open grassy areas at high elevation. That night we set up our tent at a campsite marked by cow plop. I cooked pasta and sauce, thinking we were finally near the end of our journey. I could relax as soon as we ate. Then I realized something. "Oh gee. I forgot a rope to string up the food bag," I said out loud. The night before, we had hung our food bags from the high rafters, but here, we needed a longer line. As I put stuff away after we ate, Elizabeth quietly started gathering some things out of her pack; she was working on something.

I came back from getting water and saw that she had crafted a make-shift food rope by tying together her bandanna, one of the empty stuff sacks, and some shorter lengths of nylon rope borrowed off our packs. She tied each end to two small trees near our tent. I clipped the food bag onto it. It sagged a little, but the bag was off the ground and suspended several feet away from each of the two small trees. The raccoons and porcupines probably would not get our breakfast, and I doubted we'd see a bear in this semi-open area.

The sky began to turn gray as the sun dropped low, and the three of us sat in a semicircle outside the tent door, drinking cocoa. A truly successful day was drawing to a close. Then I heard a hum, a distinct motor sound. "Girls, do you hear something?" I asked. Annie nodded. We looked toward the back of the tent. The noise got louder, and then out from the young trees emerged a four-wheeled all-terrain vehicle. A teenage boy was driving, and just behind him, a girl with long light-brown hair sat with her arms wrapped around the boy's middle.

Elizabeth's makeshift food hang.

Annie and Elizabeth set up the tent on the last night out.

My mouth dropped open. I quickly shut it. All three of us waved. The girl smiled and waved back. The boy steered the quad in a tight circle, and they headed back the way they had come. I hadn't noticed it, but a wide unmarked woods road started here, going down to another road that couldn't be all that far for an ATV but which might be far enough for a hiker to think that civilization is nowhere near.

In this night before the last night of our all-girl backpacking adventures, the sight of the ATV scared me. For the first time I realized that camping spots might feel far from other people and crime, but in fact a small ATV can cover several miles fast, just before sundown, and then turn around and return to the road before it's truly dark. The duo on the machine carried no gear, not even a sweater. This was apparently an after-dinner jaunt.

I began to think that luck, more than skill, had protected us during our trips. We had developed better skills, no question. But there we sat, settled in for the night, visited by strangers who'd motored in on a whim. They hadn't seemed threatening, but the incident haunted me. Any hiker, alone or in a group, is never truly isolated from crime, although the threat is admittedly rare. I had often scoffed at other hikers who told me they feared *homo sapiens* more than wild animals in the backcountry. But I was beginning to see their point. The ATV's visit put a little nick in my sense of security that night.

But that could not fracture the satisfaction all three of us felt the next morning when we walked out to the next road and perched against big rocks among the trees, waiting for a hiking shuttle driver I had hired. I looked at Elizabeth, who now was wearing on her head the purple bandanna she had marshalled last night to make a food-hanging rope, and Annie, whose blond hair hung down straight, framing her wide, green, intense eyes.

We had crossed Grassy Ridge, that ridge with no trees I had promised them for five years. I had made good on my pledge to get here after two failures. In that sense, I felt that I had modeled something like integrity and perseverance.

We climbed into the shuttle car. I wondered how Elizabeth and Annie would navigate trails from here. We would find ourselves moving through wild lands many more times, but never quite like this. The journey to see Grassy Ridge had concluded.

WEARING LONG JOHNS

We squeezed in our last all-girl mountain trip on an October weekend in 2003, just after Elizabeth had started ninth grade and Annie seventh. Once, Elizabeth had asked why we couldn't just go shopping instead of backpacking, so this time I promised we'd stop at the outlets in North Conway, New Hampshire. We wouldn't have to cook or set up a tent: we'd stay at Greenleaf Hut the first night and then walk unencumbered up Mount Lafayette and over the Garfield Ridge Trail to Galehead Hut the second day. Elizabeth, 14, and Annie, 12, were seasoned mountain women by now.

I looked forward to just cherishing them for the hours we'd be together this weekend.

The air felt sharply cold, and the sky was clear. We puffed up the Old Bridle Path, first alongside Walker Brook, trudging up increasingly steeper sections that turned to rock steps, hiking along the first ridge, then up more steep rocky sections, until we crossed a little low place above which loomed Greenleaf Hut. Inside, the air smelled of fresh pumpkin bread and vegetable soup. After dinner, I slipped outside in the bracing air, clustered with several strangers watching the stars for a moment.

The second morning we climbed the exposed 1.1 mile

Annie on Mount Garfield.

Annie and Elizabeth on the Garfield Ridge Trail just north of Mount Lafayette.

to the summit of Mount Lafayette. The girls had climbed this mountain at least twice before, both times in August, once with their father and me, and once with three of their cousins. The peak qualified as a family landmark. I neared the summit sign and old rock foundation and turned back to admire my daughters' coltlike legs stepping gracefully up the rock. They added jackets and winter headbands. We leaned against the rock foundation and cairns and then turned north for the 6.6-mile push down and back up Mount Garfield, then over to Galehead Hut.

Thus began a very long afternoon. I had forgotten how rugged the Garfield Ridge Trail feels on the feet. Annie looked disgusted after a while. We sat to rest and she said, "I'd like a horsey worsey to take my backer packer." We guffawed. Another hour passed as we half stumbled over the rocky treadway. Near the end, Annie cried because this trail was taking too long. Elizabeth expressed her frustration by hiking faster, getting slightly ahead.

We walked into Galehead Hut just in time for dinner. We found bunks, deposited our packs, and returned to find seats at one of the dinner tables. As we settled in among the other hikers and watched the soup and bread circulate, my daughters smiled across at me. We were in that amazing place parents and children so rarely reach: on the same level.

The fall hut croo members were working together for one last night, and they each gave introductory talks about themselves. One of the young women said that earlier in summer she had found herself telling a family she met on the trail, "Well, my parents are pirates." She guffawed, leaned her head upside down, let her hair hang on the floor, and then flung it up as everyone laughed. Here were young adults who worked in the mountains showing my daughters the joys of just feeling silly sometimes. Everyone in the hut could see that it had been a long, challenging season, and that they were letting their hair down a little on their last night, letting us see a little into their world.

I was no pirate, but I could imagine wanting to be one. Later, I wandered around the hut in my baggy pants and headlamp. I watched Elizabeth and Annie reading at one of the tables, wearing their drab long johns and fleece jackets. Maybe the next day they would find the outlets in North Conway superfluous. Maybe they would find an item of new clothing. Maybe they would remember that the person makes the clothing, not the other way around.

For seven years, the girls and I had slogged up to vistas we could see only because we were willing to walk. Each year they could go a little farther. We made it in and out of the woods together.

Once Annie remarked, "Some families go to Disney World. We go camping." Rain- and snow-covered hikes, missed turns, a few tears, many smiles. Time for deep thought. We connected with quiet companionship. And, as Elizabeth pointed out, we sometimes ate food that had fallen in the dirt.

The next morning, we walked out the Gale River Trail, caught the shuttle bus back to our car in Franconia Notch, and drove them to walk around the outlets in North Conway.

WHAT LURKS BENEATH THE VOICE OF CALM?

In the five years since the last all-girl hiking trip, Annie had become a regular hiking partner. In September of her senior year in high school, a radio reporter called me, asking if I would take her backpacking. She had read a national report that claimed backpacking was dying. I told her anyone who had never tried it was missing the intensity of immersion. So Annie and I agreed to take her on an overnight along the Appalachian Trail at the Massachusetts–Connecticut border.

For her whole life, I had led and reassured Annie when we were backpacking. Now the situation would reverse itself. At 17 years old, she could see when *I* needed help.

An hour before sunset on a chilly September Friday, we stepped upward through soft deciduous woods on the Race Brook Trail. Our companion was a radio reporter who had not been backpacking in decades. We had gotten a late start: a neighbor had backed into our car in the Cumberland Farms parking lot while we were rushing in for some last-minute provisions; then we'd crept through slow traffic on I-84 through Waterbury.

I felt confident of so much: how to get there, which trail to take, what gear we needed. I knew we could show the reporter the benefits of quiet, no technology, physical challenges, and seeing natural beauty. But first we must reach the campsite and its tent platforms and bear box, a locked metal box to keep food from black bears.

It was getting dark.

Soon enough, we could not see the path. I got out my headlamp, and Annie got out hers, and within a few minutes, the radio reporter followed us with her microphone. We were practically at a standstill, trying to find the blue paint blazes and the way up to the campsite. I tried to be the voice of calm experience. "Don't worry," I told the reporter. "As long as we stay on this trail, we will come to the campsite. We are very near it." That was true, as I kept reminding myself.

Annie, meanwhile, was positively animated. She was enjoying the dark. "This has never happened to us before!" she panted. I felt a little less in touch with my spontaneous love of the woods, especially when I realized that our companion had started recording us as we called out landmarks, turning this way and that, shining our headlamps on tree bark and yelling when we found trail blazes.

We continued upward. Soon we saw some lights inside some campers' tarp, and we stumbled up to the platforms. We were home.

The next afternoon, as we hiked along the ridge from Race Mountain to Sages Ravine, going slowly to wait for our reporter as she recorded sounds of streams, birds, and her interviews with hikers, Annie turned to me. She said that the night before during our dark stumble up trail, she was worried that I was going to panic.

"You were? Me? Panic?" I asked. "No . . . " But I could see that she was absolutely sure. I could not think of when I'd panicked in front of her. And then I realized that she knew I worked hard *not* to panic. She probably had sensed it for a while, and now she had reached the age where kids notice when the adults worry. She had her radar out the way I thought I had mine out.

There had been the time when, in the third rainstorm of our second rainy day, I'd thrown a mini-tantrum on the Appalachian Trail in Connecticut,

Annie became my hiking partner through the 2000s. Here we stand on a trip in New Hampshire in 2006. *Christine Woodside archive*

saying I was sorry to drag her out there. I'd felt responsible. There were numerous times when I'd feared we would encounter animals or the wrong people, but I had said nothing. The time near Grassy Ridge, camping in that open meadow during a thunderstorm when she was 6; the time we camped alone on the Catawba Ridge in Virginia, when I had looked warily for mountain lions; the time we camped with the man and son in camouflage jackets who had seemed a little too interested in us; the time the ATV had ridden into our campsite and I realized we were camping only a short way from a remote road because some kids had come riding through on an all-terrain-vehicle trail just as the sun was setting; the time at the Overmountain Shelter near Grassy Ridge in Tennessee, when I kept thinking I heard an animal outside. I had said nothing of my fears any of those times, but I thought things. I had known that my imagination worked overtime, and I did not allow myself to go too deep into that. My daughters were little, and I was out to prove to them that women and girls can be strong. I believed it and still believe it.

But Annie had now identified what I also know lives inside me. I'm excitable. Camping has tamed this but not obliterated it. I'm like my late father, who went with me to see the movie *Jaws* and literally jumped out of his seat when the shark first appeared.

German scientists have concluded that most cattle automatically orient themselves in a north–south direction. Czech scientists have found the same with red and roe deer. Somehow, the animals know to do this, although they alternate their heads and buttocks—one or the other points north. So they're not brilliant. They're something better: creatures that act calmly on instinct. People interested in self-sufficiency, as I am, puzzle over the instincts of animals. In the woods, I peacefully coexist with insects and other critters. When I go home, I jump at a spider and scream at a yellow-jacket. For years I feared dogs and actually fantasized about some kind of big emergency, like a hurricane, when the dogs would all get loose and wander the neighborhood. If I happen to be alone at night, I look around the house a few times to make sure no one has snuck in. But caught in the dark on a trail? That has happened to me before; the difference this time was that we had a journalist tracking us. I still hadn't thought I was panicking, but Annie knew that I was telling myself not to. Annie knew.

MAMA BEAR TO BABY BEAR: "GET UP THAT TREE *NOW*"

It's a great cliché of raising children that a mother proclaims she'd fight for her kids "like a mama bear." I've used that saying a lot. What is it about having children that makes a woman feel like Mama Bear? I *would* fight anyone who stepped between me and my little cubs. I still feel that way about my daughters now, even though they are adults living on their own.

In her mid-20s, Annie took on a project cowriting a guidebook to day hiking in the Washington, DC, area. She invited me to go on one of her research hikes. When I met up with her in Baltimore, I realized that she was feeling a little stressed out about this adventure because she had to record every detail and later write a helpful guide. This would not be a carefree day: nearly seven hours covering almost 11 miles, while taking notes. She drove us out Route 66, west and south, until trees overtook asphalt and long ridges rose above the road.

We parked at our beginning and end point of the day's long loop hike that would take us past Signal Knob, where the Signal Corps of both the Confederate and Union armies would watch their enemies' movements during the Civil War.

We began climbing a gentle but relentless slope, following orange paint blazes on small trees up the eastern side of Massanutten Mountain in Fort Valley, Virginia. As we ascended the sandy hill, the trees to our right grew thinner and the slope fell steeply away, looking like a chasm. Annie was writing on her pad, and I walked ahead for a moment or two. The trail was entering thicker woods with bigger trees on both sides. I heard rustling and a kind of blowing, whooshing sound. Something dark was moving next to a tree off to the left. It was a black bear (*Ursus americanus*)—a big black bear—and she had two cubs with her. I stood about 20 feet away. She looked over at me, and I looked over at her, and she looked agitated. She was kind of holding onto one of the cubs as she made that whooshing noise.

"Oh Annie!" I cried, "it's a bear. Let's start singing." And I reflexively launched into part of my wedding processional hymn, "St. Patrick's

Breastplate," belting out, "I bind unto myself today, the strong name of the Trinity. . . ." The bear was unmoved. We would need eight minutes to go through all seven verses! All those verses about God and Jesus and the Holy Spirit whirling around all the time, and this: "I bind unto myself today, the virtues of the starlit heaven, the glorious sun's life-giving ray . . ."

The bear blew out, loudly.

". . . the flashing of the lightning free. . . . The whirling wind's tempestuous shocks."

Annie had that wide-eyed intense look that she gets whenever her mind is going fast. I wondered if she thought I should stop singing.

I often give in to my emotions, and Annie knows that very well. Moments like this with my daughter feel as if each of us is trying to protect the other, even when we're not sure how to do it. As her mother, I want to show confidence, but with Annie, my fears come out like breathing. She would know my fears anyway, even if I tried to hide them.

We stood close, watching the bear family.

I knew a few things about bears, and I had seen black bears before. They did not scare me, but we stood so close to this one, with her babies, that we definitely were impeding her escape. I worried that she could get aggressive. I, another mama bear, even thought for a second that the bear and I might understand each other and she would realize I would not interfere with her instincts to help her children. I said, "Well, Mama, what are we going to do?"

We all stood there for a while, and I was starting to think that Annie and I should retreat, when Mama let out another whooshy sound and pushed one of the cubs up the tree, as if to say, "You get up this tree *now*. Don't you see those people over there? They don't know what they're doing."

The other cub turned away and raced down the mountain to our right, out of sight. The mama bear apparently decided she did not want to chase after the rogue child. She barreled up the tree herself, joining the first cub on a high branch.

Mama and her cub sat in the tree to our left. The trail stretched in front of us, and the other cub was somewhere on our right.

We were between a mother and one of her cubs, that classic mistake everyone says a person should never make. But we weren't actually in immediate danger. Black bear mothers make a lot of noise because they feel terrified. Of us. Scientists from the North American Bear Center call their behavior "harmless bluster, which makes them seem ferocious." Black bears do not attack in the way grizzlies in the West do. From 1900 to 2009, black bears killed 63 people in North America, and of those, only 14 of them were in the lower 48 states. Just three of the total number of killings were by mothers who had cubs with them. And according to a Bear Center report, "none of those killings appeared to be in defense of cubs." Bears that are truly dangerous probably won't run up trees and make whooshing noises. Most bears stalk prey quietly. Grizzly bears sometimes stalk humans. Black bears rarely stalk humans at all.

Black bears might bite if they feel cornered, as when a woman in Minnesota found a mama bear and her cub in her garage. The bear had nowhere to run and so came at her, bit her head, shoulder, and thighs. The woman had to have stitches. But she acted a bit like a mama bear herself: she grabbed the bear's nose and yelled at her, and the bear—true to characteristics—ran out of the garage.

Bears stand taller than I do. And they weigh between 200 and 800 pounds. But they are shy. They don't like to chat. This bear's goal was not to bother with us. She just wanted to move along and find more roots, insects, plants, and berries.

Annie on the hike to Signal Ridge.

That constant hunger, the searching for food twenty hours a day, can lead bears to campsites with spilled food or carelessly stowed food bags. If they learn that they can steal food from a certain place, they will go back again and again. They will think of it as their campsite. Some black bears, usually males, then can get very aggressive.

One time, a man at Ethan Pond Campsite in the White Mountains of New Hampshire decided to entertain Annie and Elizabeth by telling about a bear who stole his pack. Nat and I were cleaning up from breakfast by the cooking area.

"Girls, have you ever seen a bear?" he asked, and the girls shook their heads. "I put my pack down on the side of the trail once," he said, waving his arms wildly, "and a large black bear looked right at me and picked up the pack, ripped into it while I watched, and ate all my food!"

The girls' eyes widened as they silently took in this story. I wanted to punch him.

———

We stood on the Massanutten Trail, Annie and I, watching Mama Bear. Not feeling like a mama bear myself in that moment, I half whispered to Annie, "Whaaat do we do?" She said, "We're going to walk by now. Just walk by." She went in front of me and started moving past the tree. I followed her, and we continued on our way. And I realized that a role reversal had taken place. I had followed Annie.

Part III

ALONE

By Choice or Chance

From pond to pond he roamed, from moor to moor;
Housing, with God's good help, by choice or chance;
And in this way he gained an honest maintenance.

—William Wordsworth, from "Resolution and Independence"

I began to consider going alone. At first, I thought this was because my travel partners weren't as keen to go along. They wanted to do other things, and I still liked getting grubby and climbing around several times a year.

But my reasons ran deeper. I had started to feel secure enough to face nature alone. I was ready to roam and find "housing, with God's good help, by choice or chance" on my own rather than following or leading others.

On a long journey with people, we learn to care even if we're driving each other to distraction. I had learned how to give toward a group's welfare. Group hiking, though, must always focus on the group, not on individuals.

I wondered how I'd do if I were the only one on the trail. Could I rely solely on my own skills? Would I hear new sounds and encounter new ways of navigating and seeing if I were alone?

In one moment of mountain perfection with partners, captured in a photo, I began to think about when it might end.

The photo was taken at a sunny summit stop on a three-day trip through the White Mountains. Annie and I and our two frequent companions—Bob and his daughter Zoe—had just climbed to the top of North Twin Mountain. This was the second morning of a three-day circuit around part of the Pemigewasset Wilderness. In the bright sun, blueish-edged peaks rose up in the distance on all sides. We asked a stranger to take our picture. I stood

Pieces of two families pose on South Twin, July 2006. *Anonymous hiker*

with my legs bent, my arms folded in front of me. Bob straddled two rocks. Next to me stood Zoe and next to her, Annie. We were, after all, pieces of two different families, and I distinctly recall standing apart so that our families back home might not feel left out looking at this picture later.

Annie and Zoe were hiking strong and relishing the White Mountains. Our group worked hard to cooperate and boost each other's confidence. I loved that. But in the second that stranger clicked our picture, I could feel that inevitably, in the near future, I would return to this spot alone. I would cross over this very summit by myself. I would not ask anyone to take my picture then.

———————

I've hiked with many people—family, friends, and acquaintances—and partnerships have sometimes seemed perfect just before circumstances and people's preferences change on a hike that turns out to be our last time.

I was in my late 40s, feeling at the peak of my physical strength, jumping from rock to rock. I wanted to go into the mountains every month in the warm season—and stay for a while. Time in the mountains swept my brain of extraneous chatter. It showed me the world was larger than myself. I wanted to meet my ideas without distraction. I wanted to push through pain and get through to the other side. I wanted all this more often than most hiking companions seemed to, and yet I hoped that I could convince them to dream my dreams along with me.

Good partnerships are valuable . . . and rare. Circumstances must align precisely for wilderness trips. I felt lucky that so many of my group trips throughout the 2000s had combined great friends with serendipity. They were close to perfect.

I noticed that several times I—who often planned those group trips, choosing the route and figuring out the timing and logistics—found myself pushing for new terrain. My companions trusted me. I believed that they too wanted to push for more and harder experiences each time. I liked the way I felt when I moved through an area that took hours to get out of.

These companion-families and my own family unit—usually Annie and me, sometimes Nat and me—remained independent units of the others. We never cooked or shared tents with anyone who wasn't family, but we did everything else together. Our mental connection on the ridges felt like instinct. We agreed on how far we'd go. We walked at the same speed. When any of my hiker friends planned a trip and invited me along, I would rearrange my days to join them, if possible. In August 2008, Nat and the girls and I went on a canoe trip down the Saco River with Nat's brother Dave, his wife, Allison, and their three daughters. On the way back, I peeled off from the family to meet up with my longtime journalist friend Steve (who'd led the Summit New England expedition) and his son, Tom, who were partway through a bout of climbing mountains and camping.

———————

I met Steve and Tom at Zealand Campground in the White Mountains of New Hampshire. They had already been out for a few days and were peak-bagging—trying to summit as many of the New Hampshire 4,000-footers as they could on one trip. I was not peak-bagging. I wanted to walk a loop in the mountains. The next day, we hiked up North Twin, up Guyot, and on to Guyot Shelter, where we spent the night in a shelter packed with other hikers.

Early the next morning, we hiked to West Bond and across the ridge with Bond and Bondcliff. The sun shone and there was no wind. On the summit of Bondcliff, Steve said he and Tom were thinking it might be nice to backtrack by hiking over to summit Mount Garfield before going home. I said, "Why don't we hike a loop? We can go down Bondcliff and around to 13 Falls Campsite." My plan added several miles to the day and meant that we would have to camp in the backcountry another night. Steve looked dubious, but he pulled out his map and looked it over. "Well, if we do that, we could tag Galehead Mountain in the morning and then hike out." Galehead was another mountain they wanted to climb for their list. From Galehead, we could go out the Gale River Trail.

"Great!" I said. I had convinced them to do it my way. About an hour later, we were backing ourselves off the steep cliffs below Bondcliff, and the sun intensified. We trudged down below treeline into a sultry forest for miles. Finally, we decided to take a break. I swung my pack off and realized I'd just stepped on a ground nest of yellowjackets. The angry wasps rose like a cloud around us, and I started running down the path yelling. Steve and Tom moved a few feet away and reached inside their packs for snacks. They seemed bemused.

A few minutes later, we stood up and slowly lifted our giant packs onto our backs. The warm air made me think of a nap. But I roused my brain to say something friendly, now that we were in this slightly dismal part of the woods because I'd insisted we come here.

"This is great," I said, as if reminding them of the beauty of the loop hike to distract from the wasps. "We'll go around this loop now and you'll see a trail you've never seen before. I hate to backtrack." (Apparently, though, I loved to come up with plans and make others follow me.) A few minutes later, we hoisted our giant packs back onto our backs and they, smiling, followed me up the continuation of this loop I'd invented for their and my benefit, many miles through a rather gloomy forest. Finally, around 5 P.M., we emerged into the slight clearing of 13 Falls Tentsite. The quiet and distant sounds of running water did calm my soul. It was beautiful. But my loop had interfered with Steve and Tom's original deadline for getting out of the woods. They wanted to be in their car heading back to Connecticut by midmorning to get to an event in their neighborhood.

We got up at sunrise and packed hastily. We practically ran over to Gale-head Hut and up the spur trail to Galehead Mountain, adding one more peak to their list of 4,000-footers, and then we raced down the Gale River Trail to the parking lot.

On any backcountry trip, that moment of emerging safely to a parking lot combines joy and sadness. We'd made it, but the adventure was ending, and we were reentering the distractions of civilization. Immediately, Steve and I began asking hikers we'd met on the trail if they could drive us around to our cars. One of them said yes, and in we went. Steve called his wife, Lisa, to say they were heading back to Connecticut. They were going to be late for their party, I realized, but they said goodbye cheerfully and drove off a few moments later.

I thought about the previous 24 hours. I had loved seeing North Twin and Mount Guyot again, and was in awe of the blocky exposed cliffs of the Bonds, which we had crossed on a perfect day. But the part after we went down Bondcliff had us slogging many miles through static woods and swung us too far away from where our cars were parked. By now I felt a little silly for having insisted we all do a loop hike. Fortunately, Steve, Tom, and Lisa did not hold it against me.

———————

Annie's and my partnership with Bob and Zoe began as a way for Bob and me to take our daughters into the mountains. Annie and Zoe had met in seventh grade. Our family soon learned that Bob and Zoe liked hiking and that they already knew our good friend Skip, who was a photographer at the newspaper where I had worked for many years. In June 2004, just after Annie and Zoe finished seventh grade, Bob, Skip, and I took them on a five-day trip through the Adirondack High Peaks. Skip planned this loop. I had not hiked in the Adirondacks in decades and didn't know the range.

The next July, the Adirondack group minus Skip completed a four-day trip from north to south through Maine's Baxter State Park, ending on Knife Edge and the state's highest mountain, Katahdin. Zoe and Annie came alive on Knife Edge—they surged forward under a cloudless sky. I, on the other hand, did deep-breathing while alarming inclines on either side floated in my peripheral vision as in a nightmare. The young ones loved it;

they had found their legs. On a mid-October weekend, Bob and Zoe hiked with me, Nat, and Annie up Mount Flume and Mount Liberty; we paused for an overnight at Liberty Spring and then crossed the Franconia Ridge. The third year, Bob, Zoe, Annie, and I partnered up again on a three-night loop around the Pemi, covering several of the highest peaks in the White Mountains. That was the trip that gave us that photo on sunny North Twin.

The girls were strong. Bob and I agreed on routes easily. All of us hiked at the same pace.

At home, I would walk once a week with Bob's wife (I'll call her Sage). Although she didn't go to the mountains with us, she was part of the team: she packed Zoe's clothes and bought food, choosing some unusual snacks, like halvah and dried mango.

On what would be this group's fifth trip together, the summer after Annie and Zoe's tenth-grade year, Sage warned me she was a little worried about the trip this time, in a way she had never been. Our group was headed back to Maine, something the girls had said they wanted to try again. I'd chosen a new route through part of the 100-Mile Wilderness. We would start outside of Monson, Maine, and hike north. A shuttle driver would collect us on the remote dirt Katahdin Iron Works Road on our fourth day. Sage said she wasn't sure that Zoe and Bob were ready that year to do such a long

Annie (left), Bob, and Zoe on the Barren-Chairback Range.

trip. I listened but discounted the warning, thinking of our success on the earlier trips. I told her we would be fine.

Sage and I discussed the plans one Thursday morning as we walked along Great Hammock Road past the beach. We talked about which car the hikers should drive up to Maine. Sage suggested a rental car instead of risking either of our older cars, but I didn't think that was necessary.

A moment later, I found myself sobbing to Sage about how hard I had worked to set up the trip. Didn't everyone understand that? I wasn't sure why I was so emotional.

Maybe I was grasping for something that had been true the previous year but might not be so now. I could feel that I didn't just love the mountains, I *needed* the mountains. And I was hoping our team that had explored together like a strong machine would continue. A seed was sprouting in my mind, though, that attitudes change.

The next day, Nat dropped me and Annie off at Bob and Zoe's house so the hiking group could begin the long drive—in a rental car after all, to spare our older cars—to Maine. Zoe looked wistful. She spent extra time bidding her dogs goodbye.

We rode the highways and back roads for hours, in easy conversation. Annie and Zoe were teasing each other using the assigned names they'd been given for language class. "Annie-Laure!" Zoe kept calling out. We spent that night at a hostel in Monson. The hostel owner would also be our shuttle driver. She would pick us up four days later, 40 miles up the trail.

The next day, Bob parked the rental car at the Appalachian Trail crossing outside of Monson. We hoisted our packs and started walking. About fifteen minutes later, Zoe fell face-first into a mud puddle, taking the impact on her knee. She cried out that she did not want to be there. We rushed over, and Bob examined her knee. I did my best to encourage her. "You are so strong," I said as she stood rubbing her eyes.

She spent the rest of the day quiet as we stepped over boulders and blown-down logs. We made it to our first campsite, and Zoe called Sage for encouragement. The second day, we had to ford a deep stream, which took an hour. On Maine's terrain, a single mile seems like two. That afternoon, after 5 P.M., dark-gray clouds gathered overhead as Zoe stood on Barren Mountain and said she could not go on. All of us stopped. Bob quietly walked around the giant rocky expanse on which we stood and said calmly, "Zoe, there is nowhere to set up a tent here."

I showed her the map. "It's not safe to camp up here. It's only a mile to go to a shelter on a pond." Annie stood near me, silent, waiting. Finally, we all started moving together toward Cloud Pond Shelter, a beautiful spot on a remote lake. I now knew that we needed to cut short the trip. Bob had told me earlier that day that the itinerary was too ambitious. I didn't want to believe that, but I was starting to.

Even so, I argued to myself silently: It was not too ambitious for the way we had hiked as a group the previous year. But this year was not last year.

Zoe and Annie walked around the water's edge while Bob and I cooked their dinners. The storm we had feared had passed over; the setting sun tinged the air golden. I inhaled the smell of boiling noodles and began to rip open the dried cheese packet. Zoe and Annie walked back to the shelter's open front. Zoe told Bob, "Dad, I'm glad we came here." I sighed and smiled.

But I brooded over the map in my tent that night, carefully pointing my headlamp away from sleeping Annie. I knew we must scale back our mileage. The point of a hiking trip with young people is not to make them simply endure the days but to foster a love of the wilds. I reviewed the one way we could do that: get off at the next road—the only other road—sometime tomorrow late morning, saving about 15 miles and cutting off a day and a half of hiking. This would preserve our equilibrium.

The next morning, we ate breakfast mostly in silence. I mentioned to Bob that I would try to reach the shuttle driver that day if I could get a signal. I showed him and the girls the map and where I proposed we bail out: earlier along Katahdin Iron Works Road, a dirt route near Gulf Hagas. Bob nodded approvingly. So the decision was made.

We packed up and hiked into the rocky day. I fretted as I leaned into the trail. Would I find cell service anywhere in the 100-Mile Wilderness? If I couldn't alert the driver, I didn't think we should stop at the next road. She would not know where we were; how long would it take for someone to come along? Days, maybe. Or we would be marching miles on a dirt road trying to hitchhike. Would that be any better? I worried and worried.

The trail meandered up an outcropping as we climbed Fourth Mountain among tall balsams. I pulled out my phone and turned it on. A couple of bars! I called the shuttle driver in Monson and asked if she could pick us up on the next road, which we would reach today, instead of the second road, which we would have reached tomorrow.

She said, "I'm happy to meet you on that road, but I can't get there today. I can come tomorrow morning."

"That's fine," I said. We could hike the few miles to the road and camp not far from the widening of the Pleasant River known as Gulf Hagas. We'd have a fair amount of time today just to hang out, but the shuttle driver now knew where to get us.

Relief filtered through my every blood vessel as I stood on the high ledge, looking at the half-century-old forest, which had grown back after the last time a paper company had cut in this area. A forest molded by human endeavor—the old paper companies—but which still managed to look primeval.

When I caught up with the other three, I called, "The shuttle driver can meet us on the next road." Bob smiled. Zoe looked relieved. I couldn't read Annie's expression, but she seemed to relax.

We started walking the 3 miles to the road. We'd just had lunch. We were going to have a very short day, and soon we would be on our way back to civilization.

I realized, with immense sadness and even love, that our trip would end in a couple of hours. Instead of watching for moose, songbirds, and toads, pushing up the ridges with laughter and expectation, this foursome would spend its last wilderness hours together waiting by a logging road.

The woods thinned a bit. I could see the dirt road. We had made it. Now we began to separate back into our family groups: Zoe and Bob, a daughter and father dedicated to her welfare; and Annie and I, a daughter and mother who also was trip leader looking out for everyone. We set up tents in the woods slightly away from the trail crossing. Zoe climbed into her and Bob's tent, and Bob sat outside. Annie rested in our tent. I decided to hike alone up along the Pleasant River toward Gulf Hagas. It was a gorgeous sunny afternoon. I peered at swirling cool water over coarse sand, imagining sprites coming to dance while humans napped in the bright sun.

I was learning how temporal and precious is a good hiking partnership. When everything comes together, when expectations match, it's like a piece of heaven. It's a rare delight when a small group of people can walk and scramble, consider and weigh decisions, deal with what comes. But when expectations and desires change, partnerships become memories. My expectations were still going down a long path. I wanted to keep going. I felt I was ready to move beyond hoping that other people would want to go when I wanted to go.

I don't really miss the group trips so much as I inhabit them in my mind. They added a new dimension to life. We helped each other without judgment. We dodged rainstorms, shared food, egged each other on, found water, moved together through the days. It felt like heaven sometimes, but heaven is never permanent on Earth. The ground beneath us had shifted. It was time to go by myself.

HURRICANE BOB

One way I examine the ways my wild self developed is by returning in my mind to the summer of 1991. I was 33. I worked as a daily newspaper reporter. That August, a major hurricane swept into southeastern Connecticut, where Nat and I were new parents of 2½-year-old Elizabeth and 10-month-old Annie. My paper sent me to cover the evacuation of people in a nearby beach town. Then the power went out for most of a week.

That year, our baby, Annie, was undergoing a kind of reverse development in how she slept. As the months went by, she woke up more and more often. She slept in short spurts. She would not take a bottle when I was at work, which secretly made me glad, so I was happy to run home in the middle of my reporting shift and nurse her. A feeling of living fully for my baby and me. Then I'd climb back into our inherited Toyota van and careen onto

Reporting stories sent me into a joyful alter-world, where I felt total trust that my family would be safe without me for a while. Above, on board the U.S. Coast Guard buoytender Red Wood. *Staff photographer,* New London Day

I-95 and across the Connecticut River, to the two little towns I wrote about for Connecticut's *New London Day* newspaper. I'd call home later and ask Nat how he and the two girls were doing. If I could hear an edge to his voice and a sigh, I'd tense up and say, "It's all right. I'll be home soon."

I had absolutely no way of knowing whether it was all right. But I trusted.

On Monday, August 19, 1991, Hurricane Bob was coming, and the editor wanted everyone to write storm preparation stories. I called the first selectman of Old Lyme, one of the towns on my beat. How were they preparing? Would they evacuate vacationers from the beach neighborhoods? Could I go with him in his car and look at the rising water?

I diapered up Annie, made sure 2-year-old Elizabeth had her favorite books and snacks, and drove them to their babysitter Rosella's house. Rosella said, "I hope you aren't going to drive that van across the bridge in this wind."

"I have to," I said. "It will be all right." Feeling completely calm. Why, I do not know. Ignorance, perhaps. Excitement. Desire to experience the tempest. I steered onto the highway. The sky looked vaguely angry, and as I crossed the Baldwin Bridge, the van began lurching back and forth in gusts of wind. I clung to the wheel, as if gripping it tightly enough would keep the light van from lifting off.

I parked at Town Hall and slid into First Selectman Ned O'Brien's big black sedan. I had so many questions. Was it high tide yet? Were they going to make anyone leave? What if the electricity went out?

He drove the 4 or 5 miles around Shore Road to the end of Sound View Road, where a café on one side and a beachfront bar just beyond stood a few feet from the lashing waves. I'd never seen the water like this before. It was sneaky and gray, in constant motion with no pattern. I was excited. I wanted to get out and stand near it.

All I could say was "Wow." The trees were waving furiously around, and no one was out. These were the moments I loved the most in my job: witnessing an emergency while it happened and telling the world what it looked like. I did not feel scared, not one bit.

At home, Nat was back from work and he'd picked up the girls from Rosella's. He was worrying. He always worried.

I stepped into the whirling storm center of my job. At least 300 beach vacationers had fled their cottages at the urging of town firefighters and ambulance workers, who'd gone door to door. I found some of the evacuees squatting in the town's makeshift emergency shelter, the gym of Old Lyme's Center School, waiting for the storm to pass. And I started walking around from family to family, leaning down to their level on the floor to talk to them. Outside, the winds of Hurricane Bob churned. The western edge was really just brushing our coastline; most of the tempest soon would roar east and north toward Massachusetts. But even that edge of the storm was toppling trees onto power lines in coastal Connecticut.

I introduced myself to a middle-aged man leaning against a wall. His name was Greg, and his family had been vacationing in their beach house for decades. In 1954 they'd ridden out the much worse Hurricane Carol without leaving the cottage, but his mother was now 87 and he'd brought her to a medical room in the school this time. I continued my circuit. A

Looking at notes while writing a story from home in 1991. *Nat Eddy*

woman about my age glanced up from where she sat spooning soft food into her baby's mouth. She was from England and had come to Connecticut for a vacation; now she had fled the flooding roads of Old Lyme's Miami Beach neighborhood. I told her I had babies at home and asked how old hers was. "One," she said. Just a little younger than my Annie.

I took my notebook and purse and jogged out to my van. The winds were howling, but it was not raining yet. I felt so fully alive, so engaged, as if my energy had doubled with the rising hurricane. I backed up the van into the wind and drove the 10 miles home, over the bridge to the school campus where we lived in Westbrook.

The rains did not come until just after I stepped out of the van and ran up the rise to our apartment on the first floor of an old house. While Nat got the girls ready for bed, I wrote my story on our desktop computer and sent its data through the phone line to the newsroom 20 miles away. Soon after, the power went out.

The next morning, Nat pulled out our Coleman Peak 1 backpacking stove and set it up on the wraparound porch outside our apartment. For several days, we camped out that way, cooking simple meals on the porch, heating kettles of water for the children's nightly bath, and reading by candlelight. It felt instinctive, but somehow, in town, stressful too. Yet we moved through these rituals of cooking and cleaning up easily. This was what we knew.

The hurricane brought me to life in a way I had not been alive since the Appalachian Trail. I drove that Toyota van through the high winds with anticipation. I could not wait to witness the work of high winds at the edges of White Sand Beach in Old Lyme. I felt this way because I did not know what would happen. I did not know how long the storm would stay, how long we might live without electricity, and whether poles and trees would crash into buildings. I moved through that swirl of uncertainty. Wind moves as it will. We must deal with it. That I loved.

THE FOREST MERMAID

Goddard Shelter on the edge of Vermont's Glastenbury Mountain was a magic place in my memory, and five years after I first saw it, I set out to find it again.

The trail into Goddard Shelter is a tree covered route covering 9 miles. I stepped out of my family's van, pulled out my loaded backpack with tent, food, water bag and filter, clothing, and more. Lifting it up onto my right knee, I felt that weight for the first time in a few years. My muscles asked me what was happening.

———————

I'd last covered this distance with Nat, Phil, and Cay in a few hours during our AT thru-hike. The woods were rolling, unremarkable in my mind. In the late afternoon, sooner than we expected, we crossed a stream and encountered our buddy Brian coming the other way with his water bottle. "You're here!" he said. We were at the shelter early. That never happened.

We entered the clearing and there stood the shelter, almost brand-new. Its robust log walls still smelled fresh. It measured easily twice as wide and deep as most AT open-front shelters. Four fat logs held up the roof. The shelter sat on pillars made of field rocks, and it perched on the edge of a cleared meadow. A white-throated sparrow sang its clear note followed by repeated tones a third higher.

Cay cooked macaroni and cheese. We ate watching the meadow turn golden and then gray as the sun set to our right behind trees. Nat put away the food and hung the bags on the lines suspended from nails below the roof. I washed the dishes and hung the dish bag. Cay and I sat resting on the edge of the shelter and noticed a woman with long brown hair, neatly combed. She was wearing a pink cable-knit cardigan sweater and dark-blue sweatpants. She looked out on the meadow; the man she'd come with was washing dishes near the stream.

We asked her how far they were going. She smiled and said just in and out; they would go home the next morning. Her boyfriend came back from washing the dishes and the two of them silently walked down into the meadow. He said, "Would you like to go up to the fire tower?" They disappeared.

She was graceful, and clean, and her sweater was the loveliest piece of clothing I had ever seen. She was like a mermaid, except on land: she had emerged from nowhere, seemed to know something I could not know, could move mysteriously through a landscape—has anyone really seen a mermaid swim? In her case, her boyfriend had carried most of the gear and taken care of the camping, because she had never done it before.

I was dirty and stinky with months of trail living. My shorts were permanently stained where the pack belt rested. My shirt was beyond horrible. My hair was greasy. I stared at her in wonder.

————————

Now five years had passed. The fifth anniversary of the thru-hike. I was a mother of two small children, 2 and 4 years old.

I trotted across Route 9 and stepped into the woods. Within only a few minutes, light rain began falling. It might not get worse, but I took off my pack, moved my raincoat and rain pants to the top pocket for easy access, and stretched the laminated pack cover around the load. I trudged slowly and saw no one at first.

Eventually, three hikers came up behind me. I turned halfway around and gave a little wave. "Hi."

"Hey," a guy with shoulder-length blond hair said. I stepped aside and let them pass. They had a slightly dirty-stinky air, and I could tell they were long-distance walkers. I kept up with them for about five minutes. "I was a thru-hiker five years ago," I offered, "and I am just back to see this shelter again."

They took this in, had nothing to add, and disappeared ahead. I was alone for the next three hours. The rain intensified. I stopped to add rain pants and raincoat. I leaned into the inclines. At the power line, little wisps of fog completed the backdrop for this dreary experiment in solo hiking.

I concluded during that static, wet, slog that three hours in the rain feels like six hours in the clear.

There came that stream, running nicely. I was near the shelter. The rain was letting up, and I entered the opening around the shelter. In and around the shelter I saw at least a dozen men and a few women standing around, leaning over stoves, shaking out gear, leaning against the walls inside. The building was full. I would need to set up my tent.

The three hikers who'd passed me earlier were there, making their dinner. One of them, a thin teenager with dark hair, had strapped a cushioned backpacking chair to his rear end and was walking around with it. The others were laughing at him. I suppressed a chortle because I felt a little sorry for him. Could he really be a thru-hiker, hauling that thing with him? I didn't ask. I put up my tent just behind the shelter. I still remembered how to use the stove, and soon my macaroni was bubbling.

I was cleaning up a little later when the young man with the chair approached me and asked where he should pour his dishwater. "Well, I usually find a spot on the ground to pour it, away from the stream," I said.

"I wasn't sure if I should introduce a new food group," he said.

I had no answer for this.

The rain started up again, and I darted into my tent. I looked at my feet crossed in front of me. I breathed in slowly . . . and out slowly. I felt lonely.

Goddard Shelter below Glastenbury Mountain, Vermont, on a misty morning.

In the brighter light the next morning, the shelter looked darker and timeworn. It was not the magical building it had seemed five years earlier. I stepped down into the meadow and turned around. Five years before, Goddard's new log porch on stone pillars had stood tall in a misty evening. Now the misty rain obscured the dark-brown walls, and indistinct hiker chatter filtered down. I closed my eyes and imagined the young woman in her pink cardigan. The forest mermaid. She was standing with her boyfriend. They were in sympathy. They knew where they were going. She accepted (I thought) that she didn't know how to camp. She was not trying to prove anything. She had said almost nothing—and yet said everything.

ALONE WITH THE ALONE

One, two, three, four, five, six . . . I had walked 8 miles of a 30-mile loop hike in the Pemigewasset Wilderness and was taking a break to eat the peasant bread I had packed. My only other provisions were nuts and cranberries, a hunk of cheddar, and tea. I was counting people in my head: friends and family members who had once loved the mountains but had stopped coming out with me because either they had died or, for now anyway, stopped coming. I thought of the writer whose route from sixteen years earlier I was now retracing. I felt as if I'd been left playing musical chairs without anyone else to compete for the last chair. That's a lonely game, but I had chosen it, eagerly.

The day started cloudy. Then it rained. In a downpour, I crouched under a tree wearing my old red anorak that didn't keep out water anymore. I stayed low, dripping and waiting. The shower stopped, and I started up the rocky side of Bondcliff. Just before I emerged out onto the ridge, I paused and added my fleece sweatshirt underneath the soaked anorak. Wet branches drenched my arms as I climbed. Coming out of the stunted spruces, I leaned into wind gusts. A flash of blue nylon went by—my pack cover was blowing away. Then the sleep pad flew off to the right. I ran clumsily after them.

I continued on down into stunted trees and then started up the last peak of the day, Mount Bond. I felt as if I were running. My hands were numb, and I was dizzy. My heartbeats skipped, but I took my pulse and it was even. My stomach hurt. I was queasy. My muscles disobeyed. I needed food. I squatted on the rocks, held the soggy brick of peasant bread, and gnawed off a hunk.

Feeling no better, I stuffed the bread into my pack, struggled back into the straps, clipped the belt, and trudged up. Three steps and then rest . . . five or six steps, then rest again. An eerie green rock came into focus. It was a deep, true green, no more than 8 inches in diameter, and smooth. It looked like nothing I'd ever seen in the White Mountains. Could someone have imported or dropped it here? Dyed it that color? I continued the ascent. My forearms now felt wooden.

Finally, the top of Bond. It was cloudy and cold, and I could not see much beyond the rocks at my feet—so different from the brilliant, freezing sunshine on Bondcliff. I could not find the continuation of the trail, but I wandered until it emerged. I started down the last mile, eager for Guyot Campsite. Just as I had gotten into a rhythm, perhaps ten minutes later, I saw something familiar.

The green rock.

———————

Now I turned and marched like a soldier back the other way. Back to the summit of Bond. I found the proper trail this time. This was terrain I knew, but I had needed a weird green rock to guide me. My cold brain replayed this error as I tripped down to the caretaker's tent. I fumbled with the pen he handed me, signing my name. It was a big project, acting normal.

I hoisted myself onto the platform and changed into a dry top and sweater and my other coat. I just had to get the tent up. Just get the tent up, just get the sleeping bag out, just get warm. I shoved two palmfuls of my nut mix into my mouth and then carried my food bag over to the shelter to hang it for the night. My stiff claws could not maneuver the nylon cord onto the horizontal stick suspended from a rope. A man stepped over and offered to help, as many other sets of eyes watched.

During the night, I dreamed of someone asking, "What are the symptoms of hypothermia?" Confusion, nausea, exhaustion. My hike up Mount Bond, my mistake going back the wrong way, and my upset stomach all pointed to it. I wondered how I had hidden my deterioration from the shelter caretaker. Maybe I was all right. Maybe I wasn't. I shivered until halfway through the night, when finally the warmth of my sleeping bag penetrated.

In the morning, nippy air cooled the sun. I discovered, in the bottom of my pack, a black fleece balaclava I didn't remember owning. I folded it into a regular hat and stuck it onto my head. That morning, I trudged over the Twinway. I started to see a few other trekkers, young and old. Down at Galehead Hut, I spread out the goopy anorak and fleece from the previous day onto a warm rock. Inside, I bought a bowl of soup from the hut croo and

Wearing the hat that turned up in the bottom of the pack, I stand near the Mount Garfield summit. *Anonymous hiker*

talked to two young men who'd been out for three months. One of them had left his job as a hedge fund trader: "I realized I didn't care about the money."

As the light went away, hours later, I rested at the opening of my little tent on Garfield Ridge. The caretaker, Matt, who looked young enough to be my son, came to talk. I boiled water on my soda-can stove. He told me that he had fallen in love with the mountains at age 12, after his uncle dropped him off at a trail with no particular instructions and said he'd see him in a few days. Matt mentioned that a few days before, he had fed a struggling man and given him a sleeping bag. The hiker had carried no food because he was trying to lose weight. The man may not have realized, even after Matt got him settled, that Matt had saved his life.

Two days in, no sad thoughts or lost companions haunted me anymore. Something Matt said stuck with me. In winter he would hike slowly enough that he did not work up a sweat. This would keep him from getting cold as soon as he stopped. I realized that this strategy worked in summer, too. I would use it right then. Most of my life I'd chugged along like an engine. Even in the wilds, where it didn't make any difference.

The third day, I paid attention without thinking. I followed the exposed Franconia Ridge in a steady rain that started and stopped. My raincoat soaked through. They always do, eventually. I felt quite warm, though. Nothing like my first day. I nodded without speaking to a family I encountered. The overly cheerful father led his worried-looking wife and a boy and girl with their jaws set. They marched. For many years, I had led my children and other people's children on such pilgrimages. I now sank into relief. I would have myself to myself from here on.

I was walking away from the habit of thinking ahead to the next thing. The familiar rut of keeping busy. A Jesuit priest who wrote about solo retreats called the state I reached being "alone with the alone."

Time is huge, I thought. The words floated into my head as I stood on my tent platform at Liberty Spring. I would move forward propelled by the unseen inner companion from now on, despite all the memories of companions that greeted me everywhere in those white hills. Today I knew that I

On Mount Flume on the fourth morning, "alone with the alone."

could trade in those good days for something else. My father, my first hiking companion, had been gone for fifteen years. I felt his presence there on those boards. As I looked through the grainy shafts of early light, time swelled.

The next morning, I was up when the sun rose. I usually slept through that hour at home.

———————

On my last morning, I sat on Mount Flume looking back at my route. Franconia Ridge seemed to tumble behind me. Garfield stood beyond it. The Bonds saluted me from the distant horizon at the right. The sun shone gloriously. I slapped at blackflies. Then a runner emerged from the scrub, startling me. His knees were covered in mud. His glasses were grimy. His beard was neatly trimmed. He wore running trunks and carried only a small fanny pack.

"I'm doing the loop around the Pemi," he said. This was the loop I had just traversed over three days, from the other direction.

I asked, "Today?"

"Yes," he said. "Is it straightforward to get on that trail? At some point, I know I'll have to turn right."

"Yes," I said. "At some point—"

"It'll be obvious, right?" he said. "There are signs?"

I gathered myself and began to explain all the signs, all the points where he would not turn right before he would turn right. All the ways he would know when to go straight and which direction to head so that he would pass the green rock only once.

ENCOUNTER WITH A HARE

For years I remembered this moment but did not know what I'd seen:

On a July night in 1987, during our thru-hike of the AT, I awakened past midnight and crept behind the mountain shelter, over dry leaves behind the back wall. Wind whispered from the open ridge of Vermont's Mount Tom toward the spruces. I wore my improvised headlamp, a flashlight on a nylon cord tied around my head. The light wagged back and forth over dead leaves. I teetered unsteadily on my left hand while peeing.

Something rustled to the left. I turned my head. The flashlight on its cord swung out and then crashed into my forehead. I grabbed the flashlight and pointed it at a snowshoe hare. It stood giant in my obnoxious light, staring into the night. I held my breath. My companions slept. I felt alone. I did not smile or whisper, "Wow," something I might do with a person nearby. Pretensions vanished. I saw that this creature and I did not understand each other. The hare then disappeared from the edge of the flashlight's beam. Each moldering leaf near my squatting spot brightened into sharp focus.

I moved my flashlight back to my feet and gathered up my long johns. I stood and trained the light back out into the dark. The hare was gone.

Lepus americanus lives in dense forests, mostly in far-northern woods. It favors thickets. Its fur grows brown until winter and then turns white. The hare's babies stop nursing and hop off to their own lives within one month of birth. Hares spend most of their time avoiding danger. Because this one had come close, my encounter left me in awe.

———

Years later I saw my second hare, though I'm certain that many dozens of hares have watched me walk by without showing themselves. I walked alone from Carter Dome down the Rainbow Trail into the federal Wild River Wilderness. Just over the wilderness border, suddenly I noticed moose droppings every few feet. I sensed that animals hid just off this trail, waiting for me to move on.

I walked 3 miles down into desolate Perkins Notch. It looked like a ghost camp—really just a signpost. Following federal wilderness regulations, U.S. Forest Service workers had dismantled the Perkins Notch shelter about a year before, piling the lumber by the trail. Graded areas for tents now resembled rutted gravel squares. I hadn't seen one person all day. Forecasters had predicted rain. I wandered about looking for a good tentsite, not the abandoned gravel tent pads, which looked more like water collection units. I settled on a flat spot below a stand of saplings, but I felt uneasy. Something 50 yards away caught my eye. Someone had built (out of the pieces of the old shelter) a crude A-frame shack. I shuddered. "I'm not going in there," I said to no one.

The stream ran across the trail back by the way I'd come in, so at dusk I returned there with my cooking pot and water bottle. To the right and left I cringed at signs of people who'd been there and tried to erase their presence. There sat a pile of lumber from the old shelter. A rotting signpost pointed to lonely, little-traveled trails deeper in the wilds.

The stream rushed, interrupting my loneliness. And then I saw the first animal of the evening. A snowshoe hare, in summer brown fur, stood as if frozen. It stared. I stared back, fearing what it knew that I didn't know. A natural cycle in which I have absolutely no part was playing out in Perkins

On Mount Hight in the Carter Range, on the way to Perkins Notch.

Notch. The hare had emerged at dusk looking for plants it could eat in safety. An owl could swoop in and grab it. A lynx could pounce and kill it. Most hares die violently. That's why they breed like rabbits.

––––––––––

At times New England wildlife managers have transported snowshoe hares from Maine to states where too many have been hunted. Transporting hares also saves Canada lynxes because the only thing a lynx will eat is a hare. I did not worry then that a lynx might be lurking.

A hare's purpose, its movement, is completely wild. This hare looked wise. It knew what it must do always: find food, live for a while, then die. It seemed accepting of what it was. Seeing it made me feel lonely somehow. The snowshoe lives a life of worry, looking for something to eat and escaping something that wants to eat it. I could feel how disengaged I was from my own food sources. I had hauled in here what I needed to survive the night, all except the water. I was a visitor perched on this hare's land.

A wild animal lives in a constant state of fear. I have never known such fear, but I suppose I went into Perkins Notch looking for it. Theologian and backcountry explorer Martin Laird has written, "Fear itself becomes a vehicle of deeper silence," and "Be still in the midst of fear." In Inuit culture, the polar bear is sometimes called *tornarssuk,* which means "the one who gives power." One confronts the bear to grapple with fear of it and to "receive the gift from the bear."[1]

I knelt clumsily at the stream with my pot, water pump, and bottle. I could find no level ground or rock on which to prop the pump, so I lugged the pot of stream water and the rest of the stuff back to the campsite. Dusk had moved in. I could see very little. Was that movement over by the A-frame shanty? What was that crackling noise? What was that whirring sound? All potential dangers. My senses sharpened and my vision cleared. I had come out here seeking to know what I could do alone. Instead, I had confronted the gift from the snowshoe hare.

––––––––––––

1 Martin Laird, *Into the Silent Land* (Darton, 2009), a short book about Christian contemplation.

REALLY GOING OVER THE MOUNTAIN

Going up there and being blown on is nothing. We never do much climbing
while we are there, but we eat our luncheon, etc., very much as at home.
It is after we get home that we really go over the mountain, if ever.

—Henry David Thoreau, in a letter to a friend

Rain fell steadily during my solo night in Perkins Notch. I awoke just after
5 A.M., in a dim, cloudy sunrise. The soaked tent sagged barely a few inches
above my forehead. I should have known not to bring this rotting old one.
The pattering intensified. In the dark, I placed one finger and my thumb on
the prominent ridge of my nose and sighed. My father had the same nose.
Suddenly he was with me. *Dad.* The recognition flashed for a second.

About an hour later, I took down the tent and retreated into the crude
A-frame some adventurers had cobbled together from pieces of the former
shelter. Hours before, I had told myself I'd never set foot in that rickety
structure. Now I silently thanked the ambitious shelter-builders. Underneath the assemblage of tied-together logs and corrugated roof pieces, I sat
on a log bench, pushing handfuls of granola into my mouth and swatting
blackflies. As usual, I asked why my trips always came to moments like this.
I did not eat my luncheon "very much as at home." The tent fly dripped on
the rope clothesline. Maybe it would dry a little under here. A half-empty
bottle of whiskey leaned against a post: ghosts. The rain whooshed; I packed
up and set out into it.

I asked myself why, if I was so smart, I was hiking alone these days.

I came from a big, noisy family full of men. It operated on the principle
that problems resolve through loud arguments and even tantrums. Maybe
sometimes they must. But I did not realize when I left home at 18 that I'd
fallen so deeply into the family dynamic that I did not notice the emotions
and even anger with which I approached most people and all situations.

Keeping up with the boys, I had unlearned the younger me who just looked up for the planets.

I discovered backpacking during that White Mountains trip for four days when I was 24. I learned that year to stay silent, pay attention, and let the wind blow. Some people can hear their own voices amid the din of regular life. I can't. I need the mountains.

People ask if I'm afraid, backpacking alone. Sort of. But I think ahead to what might scare me, discard the unfounded fears, and take steps to prepare for the others.

Alone, I look at plants. I draw them in my notebook to remember their shapes. (Why must we know the names of things? It's the recognition that matters.) Alone, I see boot marks and animal tracks. I see animal droppings and know what the animal has eaten. When I'm alone, I see the ruffed grouse, the snowshoe hare, and the American toad. I used to let other people show them to me.

Walking out of Perkins Notch's ghost campsite, I slipped and mucked over the soaked fallen trees. I stopped for more water at the stream, now rushing faster from the rain. My prune-like hands clumsily set the old water pump on its teetering rock platform. My raincoat seemed to have taken on a new purpose as water transfer membrane. I asked myself, "What were you trying to prove this time?"

As soon as I said it, I knew I wasn't trying to prove anything. I was just getting water and living with my choices.

Hours later, sitting in the sun outside the bunkhouse at Carter Notch Hut, I leafed through a taped-up hardcover of Robert Service poems a former assistant hutmaster had left behind in 1977. "There's a race of men that don't fit in, / A race that can't stay still . . . Theirs is the curse of the gypsy blood, / And they don't know how to rest."

The poem goes on to say that those who don't fit in won't succeed in the standard sense: "it's the steady, quiet, plodding ones / Who win in the lifelong race." And yet "He's a rolling stone, and it's bred in the bone; / He's a man who won't fit in."

Absurd—that I would find my settled modern woman's soul in a cowboy poem. I didn't know how to rest. I had for a long time seen myself as one of the quiet, plodding ones. But maybe that wasn't true, and I actually needed to roll like a stone sometimes. This exercise of rolling like a stone had given me more peace, and without it, I knew I would live with regret.

This cowgirl wanted to go home for a while.

HUMAN NATURE ON THE HERD PATH

The lone ridge called Owl's Head in New Hampshire lies covered in balsam fir 4,025 feet above sea level. Nine miles from asphalt, standing hidden between the Bond and Franconia ranges, it's famous for the dread it inspires. A full day is required to reach the top of Owl's Head and get out before dark, and getting lost along the way is near the top of the list of what could go wrong. The marked trail ends a mile before the summit, at the bottom of a crumbling, overgrown rock slide half hidden by trees. The ascent reveals multiple, small, conflicting cairns, all set up by amateur trail makers. Eager feet have trampled tender plants. Blown-down trees crisscross the way. At the top of the slide, a herd path veers off. Indeed, it feels as if the fascination of the hunt for the Owl's Head summit amounts to disrespect.

Now that I was finally going to Owl's Head, I expected to be scared. Peakbaggers I'd met on other summits had told me it was lonely up there. I had put off Owl's Head to nearly the end of my list of 4,000-foot peaks. I expected bad stream crossings, muddy scrambling, and confusion at the turnoff to the slide. Appropriately, this Thursday in mid-September I'd chosen to visit brought with it a driving rain.

Jogging up the old railroad bed, I repeated out loud, "Every moment in your hiking life has prepared you for this." For trotting in 8 miles and crawling the final one; for checking the ridgeline and scouting my way up; for spending all day alone and wet. Nothing could prepare me for the reality, though. Owl's Head gained an awful reputation among people not because it's remote and unmarked and covered in fir trees, but because of the way we humans have left our marks here.

It's awful because this is what people accept until the day comes when federal Wilderness Area regulations forbidding new trails, signs, markers, and trail maintenance change, when the day comes that someone is allowed to mark and maintain a less-eroded route from a better direction.

I will leave aside my thoughts on policy. Wilderness regulations make some sense to me. I try to remember that wild lands were not created for my

Owl's Head hulks long and quiet in the Pemigewasset Wilderness, center left. Snow-covered Mount Washington stands on the horizon. *ScenicNH Photography LLC / Erin Paul Donovan*

own quests and fun. But Owl's Head amazed me. I trotted for hours to the bottom of the ridge. I smiled when I found the small cairn that, officially, isn't supposed to signal the start of the "unofficial" trail that has been marked on maps for decades. I turned up the treed-in rock slide that soon yields to an open slide and clawed my way up the loose rocks and around boulders.

The herd path slashed through mats of moss and lichen as it veered north. I could never have missed this trail unless I were dozing. It was a channel of other people's tracks. Large blown-over trees crossed the path. Otherwise, this trail that is not supposed to be there dominated. I helped it stay so.

The herd path branched into multiple scars. As I trudged along the ruts, time compressed into one wet, despicable moment. The mountain didn't ask for this. I did. I told myself that if it were up to me, I would not have slashed such direct routes into the side of a mountain deep in a federal Wilderness Area. I reached what was once considered the summit and saw the signs that aren't supposed to be there, which others had told me about, directing me to the real summit. More balsam fir trees stood in a dark opening.

I about-faced and circled around an extra loop just as many before me must have, in confusion, before diving back down the muddy incline to the rock slide. I heard high voices, and two women caught up to me. "I love rock slides," one of them said. "I've done this mountain before, but I wanted to come back with my friend!"

I watched her leap and turn, disappearing into the fog. The rain began again, smudging the deep green backside of Mount Lafayette that rose in front of us.

I woke up the next morning with a sharp pain in my right shoulder. I remembered that I had leaned frantically into that shoulder, with all of my weight, as I'd almost fallen off the rock slide on the way up. I had followed the constellation of unofficial cairns that did not mark a straight route but exerted people's need to mark their way. It was probably the most dangerous thing I'd done in a while. On the rolling boulders I had not waited for good judgment to take over because that was not a place for common sense.

Owl's Head changed me. Despite all the evidence of people who had visited before me, it was a truly wild scramble. Those two women I saw were the only humans I saw all day. And they seemed like a dream.

I asked the eternal question: why was I so compelled to finish the 4,000-footers? What was it about a list, a set of goals? From where did the urge come to compete with myself over this?

Other questions arose. Why had no one graded a more sustainable path up the other side of the lonely hill? Which is more wild: carefully graded trails or rogue trenches? I cringed at the memory of scrabbling up that scarred hillside and promised myself never to go there again. But I also cherished that terrible day because I was glad I'd climbed Owl's Head, even though I should have left it alone.

NOT A PEAKBAGGER

I told myself I did not care about peak-bagging until, in 2010, I realized how close I was to finishing the Appalachian Mountain Club's list of the 48 4,000-footers in New Hampshire.

Before that, I had clung to various admirable arguments against climbing mountains as competitive act: scrambling up gigantic piles of rock is dangerous if one puts the goal in front of safety; hiking is all about movement, not about competition; lists of peaks measure valuable experiences arbitrarily; mountains are ecosystems that support precious wild flora and fauna, not our personal playgrounds. All of that.

Until it hit me that I had become too serious.

I would lighten up, but doing so unleashed another brand of intensity. I had to admit that I had been a competitive being since age 14 when I ran my first cross-country race and sprinted my heart out to beat that boy on the opposing team's junior varsity. Competitive with others but always ready to shake hands at the end. Competitive with myself because I learned more about life that way.

The reason I had eschewed peak-bagging was that I secretly really wanted to do it.

In winter 2010, I made a list of unclimbed 48s: ten. But then I wondered if I had ever climbed Mount Monroe. I had marked Monroe as climbed in 2005—but I didn't remember climbing it.

I asked Nat and our friends Skip and Bob if during our summer solstice Presidential Range traverses we had ever stepped off the Crawford Path to reach the top of Monroe. This mountain stands just 0.3 mile southwest of the intersection of several trails at Lakes of the Clouds Hut. It would inspire poetry and song if it didn't sit in the shadow of Mount Washington, the tallest mountain in New Hampshire. Monroe rises 5,369 feet above sea level, higher than the famous Franconia Ridge peaks, and it's the fourth highest on the 4,000-footers list.

Nat said we had, but he could not remember details to satisfy my intense reporter's scrutiny of that climb. I took my pen and scratched a line through "2005" in the list of the 4,000-footers in the back of my *White Mountain Guide*.

Bob said he too thought we had gone up that year. Skip said yes but that he would check with Leigh, his daughter, who had hiked with us that year. Leigh remembered that we'd stopped on the summit to have a snack. Still, I just could not conjure an image of that summit in my mind. I was lost in the data-filling enterprise. I wanted the details. So I placed it on the list of unclimbed peaks: Cabot, Carrigain, East Osceola, Hale, Isolation, Monroe, Middle and North Tripyramid, Owl's Head, Waumbek, and Whiteface.

I made plans to finish the peaks in 2010. On June 19, while up north for work, I fit in a solo hike of East Osceola from the Greeley Pond side. On the top, I rested and watched peakbaggers, a dozen or more of them, who had come up from the main peak, Osceola (which I had climbed several years earlier, so I hadn't come that way). They trudged like zombies to the East Osceola summit marker, touched it for a second, about-faced, and marched back across the ridge. I told myself, "I'm not like that." And rested in the sun ... for about five minutes before heading back down to Greeley Pond.

In mid-August, Nat accompanied me on a hike of the Tripyramids and Whiteface. It felt great to be out in the Sandwich Range Wilderness with him, my best trail partner. He told me, though, that doing all the 4,000-footers hadn't grabbed his imagination yet. I was in full collector mode, so I planned a one-week peak-bagging and car-camping trip by myself in September.

I took the old red Subaru Outback that Elizabeth and I shared. She had used it for an internship that summer, and now it was mine to drive. On September 9, I parked at Lincoln Woods and trotted deep into the woods and up Owl's Head in the rain (see "Human Nature and the Herd Path" on p. 159). On September 10, I took an umbrella with me up Mount Hale, a smooth trip to a wide, gravelly opening with a giant cairn. On September 11, I met my friend Sally Manikian for a hike of Mount Cabot. It was a beautiful sunny day. On September 12, I climbed Waumbek via Starr King Trail. I saw no one that day.

On September 13, I sat on the gravel by the red Subaru in the Rocky Branch parking lot off Route 16, leaning against the metal door. I was tired of hiking. I wanted a day off. But it wasn't raining, and Mount Isolation was only a few hours' trot away. I was there, after all. Then only one peak on the list (maybe two, if I counted Monroe) would remain unclimbed, and I'd be meeting Skip and my friend Martha in a few days to tackle Carrigain. So I hiked in the slight fog up Rocky Branch, to the Davis Path, and then hoisted myself to the remote, dreamy summit. I couldn't see far beyond my feet up there, but the mossy expanses around birch trees on the Davis Path made me gasp with happiness. I propped my camera on the top and managed a blurry shot of me standing in my black raincoat. I was alone. I didn't have to smile. I knew I felt content. Then I skipped down, down, down, across the seven streams and back to the car.

The next day, I drove to the Cog Railway Base Road and the Ammonoosuc Ravine Trail. Clouds hung on the summits. As I steered up through Crawford Notch, the clouds wisped their way in and out, hiding and then revealing the fuzzy green and rocky profiles of Mount Willard and Mount Webster. I gasped and tears pooled in my eyes. It was so beautiful I thought I needn't even get out of the car. But I must climb Mount Monroe. So I drove on, turned off onto the Base Road, and parked at the trailhead. I strapped my pack over my raincoat and rain pants and set off. The trail is relentless but efficient, and I told myself that I was definitely going to summit Monroe at last, instead of bypassing it as I had so many times. I pushed and grunted up the wet rock slabs below Lakes of the Cloud Hut. The misty rain seemed to be rising from the ground near the hut. I made out the sign marking the final 0.3 mile to Monroe, but first I wanted to warm up and eat something.

Inside the hut, the AMC Construction Crew was closing up the building for winter. Boxes were everywhere, and workers were hammering covers over windows. They told me I could rest there for a minute. I shoved a slightly crushed peanut butter sandwich into my mouth, glugged some water, and then added a fleece under my raincoat.

Back outside, I stood by the sign for a second and then headed in the direction it pointed. Immediately, visibility was only a few feet. No cairn showed in the mist. Monroe had disappeared into the cloud. I hesitated, trying to decide whether I should push into the soupy air, and then I knew that I could not press upward. I might get lost and stumble around in the grip of a lonely mountain for hours, maybe getting stuck in Oakes Gulf. No. I turned around and slid my boots onto the damp rocks below the hut, descending into the gloom of Ammonoosuc Ravine. I had failed to summit Monroe.

The next day I took off from hiking. It was pouring rain. I met Skip that night at the Dry River Campground; we'd join Martha at the Signal Ridge Trail the next morning. As the sun set, a moose tramped by behind us. We were the only people at the campground, and it felt like a wild place. The next day was cloudy, but we got up Carrigain with no problems and lingered on the fogged-in observation tower. I remembered that mountaintops are ethereal even when you can't see anything. All three of us were smiling. Skip and Martha asked me how I felt. Wasn't it great to climb all the 4,000-footers?

"Yes . . . Well, I'm not sure if I'm done. There's Monroe," I said. "I just can't remember it."

The next year, 2011, the mountains felt out of reach. My mother-in-law died, and we had a large family reunion around her burial that summer. I took a long trip to Iowa researching a book. I didn't have time to go back to Mount Monroe.

On July 11, 2012, I parked at Pinkham Notch. I approached Monroe from the other direction this time, from Boott Spur Trail to Davis Path to Tuck Cross, and felt as if I were traversing heaven. I reached the junction of trails by the hut and scrambled up, stopping every minute or so to turn around and admire the view of Washington rising behind me. The top of Monroe felt to me like a giant rock shelf at the edge of the Presidentials. I savored it and then went back the way I came. My list was complete.

———————

Epilogue: In December 2022, I awoke from a dream. I could hear my own voice back in 2005 saying to Bob and Skip, "This year, instead of bypassing most of the summits on our traverse, let's take the extra half hour and go up!" We summited Jefferson because of this speech. And a few hours later, we summited Monroe. I remembered it now.

MY SECRET LEDGE

A certain ledge in Cockaponset State Forest, a few miles from my house, gave me refuge during most of 2020 and remains the local place where I sort things out. I walk to the end of my road and trudge up old woods roads into the state forest, stepping over ruts where long, narrow puddles linger in dirt bike tracks. All around, rock ledges left from the last glacial retreat rise up. Boulders are my favorite aspect of Connecticut. They have sat there for about 25,000 years. They seem to wait for that time when the rounds of storms and temperature will heave them up again.

As soon as the COVID-19 pandemic quarantine started, and it seemed that half of the population had started walking on the woods trails, I began retreating into this tract of forest near my house, avoiding busier paths.

In rural Deep River and Chester, in the lower Connecticut River valley, the chances that I'd run into big crowds were low. Yet I sought a wilder patch of backcountry. I quelled my anxiety over what social distancing could mean and what the then-novel coronavirus could do. In mid-March 2020, scientists were just beginning to study the virus. They weren't sure all the ways we could catch it or give it to each other. The government's best advice resembled that of the flu pandemic in 1918: stay away from other people, step back if we encountered anyone, and, eventually, cover our faces if we did see anyone.

And so I would slip away—retreating into a dreamlike world I found in that oak and beech forest. This expanse is nestled west and south of Route 9, crossed by dirt roads. I started going regularly to a certain ledge there. It is by no means an unknown place to the locals. We just don't publicize it.

———————

I walk in the woods for many of the same reasons other people announce that they do: I love peace and quiet of deciduous and pine woods. In Connecticut, thousands of miles of marked trails meander through the Connecticut

River valley. I like trees. Their canopies give creatures homes and shelter me from real and imagined storms in my own life. I love glimpsing wildlife—a wild turkey, a hawk, or a coyote. They always run away from me, and that's humbling. My presence bothers them more than they can scare me. I smile at the ubiquitous chipmunks moving in fast-forward time. And robins start their crazy, loopy songs almost every time I go out. If I walk with human companions, I know that out there we will get to the heart of things faster than on a busy road. We will speak honestly instead of chattering.

But I also hike for deeper reasons. I go to figure things out. On the trail I don't need words to know anything. I watch without any expectation of what will emerge. The great Connecticut walking-trail expert Eugene Key-arts once wrote, "At first one must learn the art of seeing, not just looking." He wrote the little handbook *60 Selected Short Nature Walks in Connecticut*, long out of print. Each walk got two cryptic pages and a hand-drawn map. Keyarts described how to get to each hike and what the trail looked like. Then, without a break, he let his mind wander to whatever he wanted to tell readers. He might write about the mighty oak tree and its protein-rich acorns or describe a dragonfly scooping up an insect on a pond's surface—only to be eaten by a frog. Or he'd criticize humans for our natural tendencies to litter and rampage. Keyarts and his humble green-covered paperback guide gave me my first glimpse at the extensive trail networks in this little state, to which I relocated at age 28.

I hike in the woods because sometimes I don't know what my priorities are, and there I can think without distraction. Maybe I want to grasp how I really feel about something someone said or map out the route I'll take to fulfill an obligation. Maybe I just feel unspecified monsters stirring in my mind. I hike because my personal landscape emerges on the dead leaves of last year's growth.

Hiking out to my ledge in 2020 mimicked the transformation the pandemic brought to the wider world. I realized that these hikes were not a diversion, just as the coronavirus would be no temporary visitor. In fact, society changed that spring, and it will continue changing. People no longer seem pulled from home if home will suffice. I'm different now, too. I won't wander into a noisy roomful of people unless I have a good reason. I've

A pitch pine grows toward the light at the edge of the secret ledge in Chester, Connecticut.

divided the phases of my life in two: the time before the pandemic and the time after. That spring, I crossed a line into the new reality as I hiked over the rolling dirt tracks to my ledge. And I realized that I could learn to navigate the post-pandemic world and to help those I love do the same.

———————

I was not the only one who climbed up to that ledge. I saw evidence of climbers who'd inched their way up the front of it and partiers who sat on top burning brushwood fires. We weren't that many, and I rarely overlaped with anyone, so that place felt personal. It was big enough to share and still feel alone. Whenever I climbed the last few yards to the top and saw the skinny, twisted pitch pine branches hovering over the precipice, I felt as if I were interrupting a meeting of sprites.

I felt that the place knew and understood me, and that comforts me to no end. A lot about the world of recreation and exploration has changed and will change. With the pandemic, the meaning and purpose of hiking to a destination in the backcountry altered for me. Hiking was no longer pure recreation but a balm to a soul on edge. For most of my adult life, I explored the woods of Connecticut to connect *and* to recharge. Then I chose a place where the connections were all wild. Where no one would speak in language. My ledge does not feature in published hiking books. It's not on any list of top destinations.

On my ledge, time passed on a different scale because the way I experienced it during the world's quarantine silence fell out of expectation or measure. Getting there, I tried not to match ground covered to minutes on a Global Positioning System (GPS). I avoided marking time on the clock out there, too, but I usually failed at that. Returning to a secret place over and over narrowed my vision and focused understanding into one outdoor universe four stories high, higher than any other nearby ledge or building. I thought it all through: I was lucky. I was healthy and still had work, and so did Nat. Our two grown daughters, living that spring in California and Maryland, were holding on well. I worried about them the way mothers worry, but I mainly just felt love for them and thought of ways to express it from a distance. I trusted that they would be OK.

From my ledge, during the early months of the pandemic, I heard wind in the trees, and birdsong. The highway less than a mile away normally hums with traffic, but for ten weeks, I heard no distant car and truck motors. That silence said that hundreds of thousands of people in my region could not go to work; that many had lost their jobs; that residents were struggling to pay bills and get food; that children and teenagers could not go to school; and that all the normal channels to help people—therapy, churches, synagogues, mosques—had shut. In that silence a heavy weight hung over Connecticut. A new disease had afflicted tens of thousands of people and by mid-May of 2020 killed 3,449 of them in my state. By spring 2023, 1.3 million Americans had died of COVID.

Pitch pines grow on my ledge. They love dry, sunny places like sand plains, but most of the sand plains in Connecticut have disappeared beneath buildings and malls. The pines grow slowly on ledges that face the sun in just the right way, waiting patiently for what they need, clinging to rocks and sliding their roots around to get a purchase. These trees make up 0.04 of 1 percent of the Connecticut forest and less than 1 percent of all the pines in the state. They are a relic of another time, when they grew more abundantly and when people cut them down for their resin-filled knots where limbs meet trunk. They were known as candlewood because those knots would start fires so neatly.

My hikes in there proved that moving through nature heals. I love to quote Belden C. Lane, a theology professor and backpacker who wrote in a book about the spiritual side of wilderness hiking[1] that just "plodding an uphill trail" migrates his mind away from panic and impulsive thoughts or actions. Lane knows that moving through the woods "evokes an intuitive way of knowing. . . . What the mind hardly fathoms, the body already knows."

Walking into wild places is an act of faith. I don't feel afraid in the backcountry because I'm used to moving through it. I knew that bobcats might be denning somewhere near this ledge; from up here, they could see their prey: hares, turkeys, chipmunks, raccoons. In spring, green and sometimes reddish buck moth caterpillars chomped on oaks until they metamorphosed into huge black-and-red-winged creatures. Maybe I had inadvertently stepped on brownish, slimy Gerhard's underwing moth larvae as they munched on roots. The grand theater of nature hid just off trail when a human breezed through. I was just a visitor for a moment. Once this might have scared me. Now I feel glad I can visit this mysterious world for a while.

---

1 Belden C. Lane, *Backpacking with the Saints: Wilderness Hiking as Spiritual Practice* (Oxford University Press, 2015).

In spring 2020, isolation felt like a community act as people everywhere suffered in the same ways. Millions of people got sick with COVID-19. No vaccine or medicine could help. Populations shut themselves away or went about business tentatively, looking away from each other or crossing the street to keep their distance. For a few weeks, the ordeal felt temporary, but then people began to understand that this threat and our inability to stop it would not be resolved quickly. The pandemic would retreat over many months, and the virus that caused it would be with us forever while humanity struggled to detect it, treat it, or avoid it.

At some point during the ordeal, the truth rose up through all the little irritations and challenges of it, and I knew that I would emerge on the other side less restless, willing to cope with sudden illness, changed plans, and semi-isolation. The pandemic changed me.

The first time I learned how challenges strengthen was the year of my thru-hike of the AT with Nat, Phil, and Cay. We slept on a different floor or piece of ground every night from mid-April through early September. Our feet, backs, knees, and shoulders ached every day. Everything about this trip was hard. I jumped over and slammed onto rocks, mud, roots, and pavement. My feet were bruised, my shoulder blades hurt all the time from 35 to 45 pounds on my back. I smelled bad, and my gear smelled worse. It seemed, then, that we were slogging through hell—and by choice. It would have been funny except that it was so painful.

Early in the pandemic of 2020, I felt a little like that. On those rare days when I had to venture out in my car, if one other vehicle showed up in the rearview mirror, my breath would become shallow and my forehead knit with tension. In the supermarket, I'd step away from the canned tomatoes, making room for three others who also intended to make spaghetti. "Sorry," I'd say, "Sorry." Everyone seemed like strangers. I felt strange. I didn't know where they'd been, and they didn't know where I'd been. Just breathing the same air made all of us want to take a number as if we were waiting at the motor vehicle department.

But the story didn't end with that. On the Appalachian Trail journey all those years ago, somewhere around two and a half months in—say, around early July—I knew that I had changed permanently. I knew what I was doing. I was used to living that way, homeless and with just the basic necessities. Water from a spring and a simple meal were now all that I needed. I also knew that my companions and I would change more over the next two months before going back to society. I never looked at a water spigot the same again after that trip.

That's where I was in spring 2020. My secret ledge helped me change. Daily I thought about happy and beautiful things, clung to routine, did work I love, felt thankful for health, work, money, food, family, and friends. Society somehow was handling it. I think I could do that because I had the freedom to walk into the woods, to the quiet places . . . and especially that big rock.

Part IV

FORWARD

On Little Haystack Mountain, Late in the Day

O n a late afternoon in June 2003, on our Adirondacks High Peaks circuit, Bob, Zoe, Skip, Annie, and I reached Sno-Bird Campsite just off the State Range Trail. We had climbed a lot that day and were tired, but the sun was still shining. After we'd set up our tents, Skip asked if anyone wanted to backtrack a bit and try to go up Little Haystack. We'd bypassed the trail to it on the way in, and Skip was intrigued.

"I'm never going to be here again," he said. He was in his early 60s. It was not a fatalistic remark. The Adirondacks were not a range he normally visited. He wanted to see other places; this was not going to be one he'd get back to. He prized his guidebook to the Presidentials in the White Mountains. His focus tended toward New Hampshire.

He nodded with certainty. "I'm never going to be here again. Let's go."

Annie and I said we'd take an amble with him. We grabbed a water bottle, Skip got his

Skip taking pictures, this time on Mount Madison in New Hampshire.

179

camera, and the three of us stepped back up to the State Range Trail, walking 0.3 mile to the turnoff for Little Haystack. The sun was getting low, and we climbed the open rocks until we all decided we'd better turn around.

Skip took some photos of me and Annie in our long-sleeved tops in front of shadows playing on the ridges. I put my arm protectively around her, as if to say, "You're all right." I hoped I did that enough.

Later, Skip remembered he'd left his camera cover somewhere on that ridge. But what stuck with me was that he got us up there, a spontaneous little scramble. We didn't reach the 4,662-foot Little Haystack summit, but that didn't matter at all. You may never be somewhere again. Grab hold, appreciate the moment.

STRAIGHT UP

One beautiful August morning, as sunlight cast splotchy shadows onto the rock highway of Tuckerman Ravine Trail, I failed to save a man's life.

I trudged alone in a crowd up the most popular trail on New Hampshire's tallest peak, Mount Washington, heading for the Alpine Garden just below the summit. I'd never seen that section of the mountain before and looked forward to walking near the tiny-leafed plants, even though their flowers had already come and gone for the year.

I caught up to a 40-ish man walking with his young son. "Hi—we heard you talk last night," he said. I had given a little after-dinner speech at the Pinkham Notch Visitor Center. We chatted a bit about my message, which I called "Straight Up." It discussed why trails in the Northeast's most jaw-dropping range tend to blast straight up the mountains rather than follow gentler switchbacks. We were huffing up one of those straight-up routes right now.

We stopped talking and returned to just breathing and ascending. I got ahead and didn't see them anymore. The trail swung wide about 2 miles up from the trailhead. People were in front of me and behind, and in the middle of the trail we came upon a commotion. A young man was shouting, and two others were leaning over a figure lying on the trail. All I could see were black sneakers, white socks, pale knees and calves, khaki shorts. All very still.

One of the helpers, who identified himself as a nursing student, pulled something out and yelled, "I have an EpiPen!" He was counting loudly. Another man pounded on the still man's chest while the third man blew air into his mouth. "Does anyone know CPR?" he called.

"I do," I said quietly, stepping close.

At least I thought I still knew it. I suddenly remembered a movie I'd seen in the CPR class I'd had to take years ago when I was training to be a lifeguard. One of the people interviewed said she'd saved someone using techniques she'd learned decades before. The film narrator told us we would never forget, either.

Other hikers stepped up and offered to help. The nursing student fashioned a mouth guard out of a latex glove. I leaned close to the still stranger, my face inches above him: a clean white T-shirt stretched over his slight potbelly, his face was round and clean-shaven, and his dark hair held a few strands of gray. I took my turn blowing air into his mouth and then pushing on his chest. (This was several years ago, before cardiopulmonary resuscitation practices changed to chest compressions only.) I found myself falling into the rhythm of a desperate lifesaving act with a handful of men and women I'd never met until then. We tried to push life back into him. I could not tell if the man was responding or if I was just hoping I saw color in his face when air entered his lungs.

A half dozen of us rotated work: first compressions, then blowing into his mouth, then resting. Men and women of all ages stopped and helped. I spent many minutes blowing hard past that latex. The air went in, but it seemed to do nothing for him. We knew the odds were small he would survive, but we didn't try to guess. We just pumped and blew as minutes stretched into an hour. He did not move.

We all walk along in life carrying burdens, most of them of our own invention, looking for meaning. I'd gone out there that morning hoping to connect with the essential me, as I always do on mountains. Now this urgent business occupied my entire mind: saving Mr. M—., whose identity I would not learn until later. His teenage daughter, I soon realized, sat nearby on a rock waiting as we did our work, and whose other daughter, I later realized, I'd passed on my way up chatting with that father and son I'd met. The older daughter had been running downhill against the tide of climbers.

A caretaker from Hermit Lake Shelters came running toward us, hauling a defibrillator on his back. One of the lessons I remembered from my long-ago CPR training was that in the backcountry you keep going with the compressions until someone with more training tells you to stop. We stood by for three or more rounds while the caretaker tried to jump-start life. Then we resumed. He walked several paces away and called the hospital, his back turned. A moment later, he came back where we stood. He said we had done our best. We had tried, but we must stop now.

I couldn't leave just yet. A few of the hikers had sat with his younger daughter during the ordeal. I stepped over to her and sat down. I tried to tell her we had done everything we could. She stared off into the shade. I moved away out of respect.

We dispersed. Some hiked up. I went the half-mile to Hermit Lake, paused at the fence, looked up at the rock bowl below Washington, and then headed down. This was not a day for the Alpine Garden.

Outside Pinkham Notch Visitor Center, I ran into Mike Micucci, a seasoned search-and-rescue volunteer who sometimes worked the desk at Pinkham. I told him what had just happened. He peered thoughtfully at me. "Don't try to do anything too important the rest of the day." He said these traumas take a while to sink in. He obviously understood well the emotional hangover that results in trying for hours to save someone who dies.

A few days later, I posted a condolence letter on the funeral home's website, introducing myself as one of the hikers who had tried to save Mr. M—.

His sister emailed. "Can you tell me any more about what happened?" she asked. We were going to try a phone call, but after a few days of silence, she emailed again. She was sorry, but calling was too overwhelming. Could I write what happened? So I wrote an email. One of the helpers had been a nurse. She had told me that he had likely felt no pain. I relayed this to the sister. I hoped that Mr. M—.'s last thought might simply have been that he was on Mount Washington on a stunningly gorgeous August morning with his daughters at his side and his wife waiting below.

Several days later, a small card with flowers in its corners came in the mail. The sister had handwritten her thanks, grateful for the few details I could share.

Sudden death at age 57 a few miles from a road. He was a year older than I was. Was it the biggest mountain in New Hampshire that led to his collapse? One can never know. He could have collapsed almost anywhere. How and when people die can be hastened by choices—or not. How we live determines (at times) the quality and length of our days, but fate can intervene. I have spent my entire adult life trying to avoid a premature death because my uncle, grandfathers, and father all died of heart disease. One June afternoon a few years after Mr. M——. died, I suffered heart palpitations and dizziness on a small mountain I had climbed very quickly after work. A week later I found myself on a cardiologist's treadmill, resting my hand on the nurse's shoulder as she took my blood pressure. I was fine for that moment, but a few years later I needed outpatient surgery for my unpredictable bouts of the heart. The problem went away. I felt lucky.

I wrestle with what happened that day on Mount Washington. I learned something about myself: I had not hesitated to help. Until then, I hadn't known whether I had the courage, but all of us are capable of things we aren't sure we can do. The team on the rocky incline worked in harmonious purpose. Most of us would never learn each other's names. But we did know each other briefly during that moment of doing what we must do.

MEMORY FAILS, LOSS MAGNIFIES

In 2011, a few months apart, two people I loved died. One day my mother-in-law shooed me away as I tried to help her stand; soon after, she lay in the hospital. One day our friend Bill laughed raucously at my joke; soon after, an ambulance carried him away from his house. And for good measure, my poodle, Charlie, whom I loved beyond love, was taken with seizures. Within 24 hours, he was watching me dig his grave, and then he was gone.

Melancholy sharpens the edges of vision. The sting of loss measures the beauty of those three. I see clearly what's lost now.

Gretel Ehrlich wrote, "Loss constitutes an odd kind of fullness; despair empties out into an unquenchable appetite for life."[1] But last year all this dying—and, admittedly, some boundless joy, like my daughter's college graduation—left no time for my usual backcountry trip. I could not get away and so could not find my way back.

In November, I sat by the woodstove reading through my old manila folder of crumpled diary notes from prior backcountry trips. I came upon a scrawled entry from several years ago: I'd returned to Cow Camp Gap, a shelter I'd remembered clearly from the AT thru-hike, previous trip but found nothing familiar. (See "The Camouflage," page 93.) It lay in a small clearing below a gently sloping ridge, surrounded by ash, oak, and maple. I had remembered a grand, light-yellow, capacious shelter, luxurious by trailside standards. But on that second visit, when I ducked in under dark, weathered boards, it was obvious that even though the boards had weathered from their original yellow gleam, I'd prettied up my memory with a larger, airier space.

The shelter turnoff from the Appalachian Trail in Virginia I'd remembered as a treed-in, short path, with a gentle grade. Revisiting, I found it a

---

1 Gretel Ehrlich, *The Solace of Open Spaces* (Penguin, 1986).

narrow trail that swept steeply downhill into Cow Camp Gap. The ridge actually dwarfed the little building, which was no grand, clean oasis at all. The first time I'd trudged through there, I had arrived after walking across ridges for two months, and I had ceased noticing the oaks, grass, ferns, and rocks. I had fallen upon anything civilized that differed from my daily trail life. I had minimized the mountains and maximized the buildings.

Surprised by how minuscule the camp really was, I wondered if I had connected with the natural world at all, the first time. Often, even today, when I'm in the mountains, I feel that I don't fit in, that I'm different from a bear or snake. And yet I felt when I returned to Cow Camp Gap—and still feel now—more at home in the mountains than anyplace else. This ought not make sense. It's like loss. Lose people and love them better. Look back in nostalgia for what you could not see when it stared at you. Leave home and yearn for it. Return from the mountains and forests and wish for them. That's living well.

THE DEATH OF GERALDINE LARGAY

On the morning of July 22, 2013, Geraldine Largay hiked with her full back-pack along a rugged stretch of the Appalachian Trail south of Stratton, Maine, on her way from one backcountry shelter to the next. She crossed Orbeton Stream and walked over an old railroad bed. She stepped off the trail to make a pit stop in the woods.

Then she got lost.

Teams of ground searchers and search dogs with their handlers tried to find her for two years. A forester surveying adjacent land owned by the U.S. Navy stumbled upon her flattened tent, strewn gear, and remains in October 2015, nearly 3 miles from where she'd first stepped off.

The Maine Warden Service hiked in the day after the forester's discovery. They found a diary (not made public) and some notes to searchers. They found her food wrappers, her clothing, and her cell phone. She had waited in that tent under dense tree cover instead of moving to lower ground, where she would have been more likely to find her way to roads and people. She had been alive when the first major search ended. She might have lived almost a month after she was last seen. What went through her mind as she waited to die remains a terrible mystery to most of us.

In 2016, the Maine wardens released thousands of pages of data from the search. These pages took me many weeks to read. They tell of the ground searches that led to nothing and reports of false leads. Hikers and the public wrote and called: they blamed Bigfoot; they thought they had seen Largay in restaurants or hostels months later, even places many miles from Maine. For a while, a sensible theory suggested that she might have fallen off a cliff. Some people were sure she'd been killed or abducted. Her cell phone number was taken over by someone in Illinois; the investigation into that took many days.

In these documents, a few crucial clues to what happened jumped out at me. In the end, her death was the result of her own decisions. My heart grieves. I cannot get this tragedy out of my mind. It has taken over my late-night musings. I read and reread the pages, hoping that I will find some explanation of why a strong hiker who'd been on the trail for three months was unable to walk herself toward a woods road or streambed.

This tragedy unfolded not because of bad weather or terrain, failure of equipment, or lack of hiking experience. Gerry Largay was used to rain and rough terrain, she had top-of-the-line equipment, and she had hiked 950 miles. This tragedy developed because she was terrified.

As a woman who has backpacked solo many times, I feel invested in showing that women can survive getting off course. So I might look harder in the documents than most people for some clue that the reason Gerry Largay got stuck was that she encountered bad luck that no strong person could have overcome. I find something darker. I find fear.

For more than two months, she had hiked with a partner, her friend Jane Lee. Lee had to leave the trail at the end of June for a family emergency and asked Largay to wait until 2014 to finish. Largay said no: she and her husband, George, who was driving from point to point and helping his wife resupply, had moved out of their house in Atlanta, Georgia, and stored their belongings. They had a great deal invested in Gerry's doing the hike that year.

Largay wanted to continue despite the fact that she disliked solitude on the trail. Lee told investigators that Largay feared being alone so much that she would go to great lengths to avoid that by hiking farther to a shelter where others would be instead of camping by the side of the trail.

In one affidavit, Lee "stated that Geraldine routinely would become disoriented throughout their hike and they would have frequent arguments about which direction to hike in along the trail . . . as the terrain became more difficult Geraldine became more easily disoriented."

Maine's terrain is rough and slow going. Largay's progress was about 1 mile an hour, which is normal for many through that stretch. On July 22, 2013, she left the Poplar Ridge Shelter at 7:15 A.M. and texted George, who was meeting her at the next road a day later: "About to leave shelter. Don't worry about getting stuff for 100 Mile Wilderness." This message suggests to me that Gerry Largay was considering a break. She may have been rethinking her decision to hike solo because the terrain had become so challenging.

By 11:01 A.M., she was lost. She composed the following text to George, which he never received due to bad reception: "In somm trouble. Got off trail to go to br. Now lost. Can u call AMC to c if a trail maintainer can help me. Somewhere north of woods road. XOX." She tried to send this message ten more times.

The next day, she wrote this text: "Lost since yesterday. Off trail 3 or 4 miles. Call police for what to do pls." She tried to send this again four days later. She apparently composed and sent other texts, none of which made it out.

Lee told investigators, "George doesn't know the extent of Gerry's inability to deal." But she was sure that her friend would not have gotten lost at the trail intersection near where she went missing. The AT is well blazed in that section.

But I believe that because Largay was alone, she went farther off the trail than usual for her pit stop, taking her pack with her instead of leaving it on the trail. Thus, an act meant to keep her safe ended up putting her in danger. From there, things deteriorated because, according to the police notes, Lee said that Largay "didn't know how to use [a] compass." That she had "no confidence." That she had phobias: "alone, in tent, dark." And so, after she got lost off-trail, she must have decided to set up her tent under great duress.

Gerry Largay also took various medications that she needed to keep taking; if she ran out, she would have had reactions that could include panic. The reports didn't specify the amount of medication she had with her, but Lee told police her practice was not to carry anything extra. It's clear that she was not set up to wait long in the woods without running out of medication.

The evidence points to this: she decided early on that if no one could find her, she would die at that site. I think she gave up within the first few days and started a waiting game. This must have been excruciating. But fear can be a powerful fixative.

Rescuers found a diary and a page from a book with writing. They did not make the diary public. But the page from the book, dated August 6, said, "When you find my body please call my husband George . . . and my daughter Kerry . . . [it] will be the greatest kindness for them to know that

I am dead and where you found me—no matter how many years from now. Please find it in your heart to mail the contents of this bag to one of them."

She made the decision to remain in situ in impenetrable forest even though she had a loving family desperate to find her. How I would like to become a genie and turn the clock back, visit her, and urge her up and out—downhill toward a streambed or the nearby railroad bed she'd crossed. How I would like to talk with her and discover what she was thinking. I believe that this is a textbook example of why staying put and waiting is sometimes a very wrong decision when the chosen site is so obscure.

"I wish you were here," wrote her granddaughter in capital letters on the wooden cross her family placed at her final resting place. Everything we know about her from her family says that Geraldine Largay would have wished that, too. Except that for some reason, she was unable to save herself.

PEAKBAGGER

Ellen and I first bonded as editors of our high school newspaper, *The Tower*. Our responsibilities often seemed too much for two teenagers: molding ideas into articles, opinions into editorials, lists into deadlines. Searching for lost notes, rewriting stories at the last minute, and coping with a principal who abruptly cut back our publication schedule, she and I always managed to laugh about the absurdities.

We ran into each other at our 35th reunion of Princeton High School. She told me she had recently begun a quest to summit the 48 New Hampshire 4,000-footers and had completed five so far. I had finished my 48th two months earlier. She asked if I'd go with her on a hike in October; I said sure. We had never done anything like this together.

When she asked about hiking the 4,000-footers, I saw she had physical strength and a sincere desire to complete the list. Her inspiration was newspaper reporter Tom Ryan, author of the book *Following Atticus* (HarperCollins, 2012), a story of hiking the 4,000-footers with his miniature schnauzer, Atticus. Ellen wanted to do the same with her dog. The boulder-strewn trails in the fierce little White Mountains present different challenges than pavement does, and she had not explored this high terrain much yet. She wanted a companion, and I was glad to help.

In high school, Ellen was quiet and studious. Her wavy auburn hair hung below her shoulders. She was long-legged and tall, liked wearing blue jeans and Fair Isle sweaters, and pursued sports privately off campus. She rode a unicycle and once a year would perform with other unicyclists in the annual variety show. She took long bike rides with some of our friends. She ran long miles on her own, too, but I didn't know about that until years later.

I also ran in high school, competing on the track and cross-country teams for a few years. As a freshman, I finished seventh in New Jersey in the mile. But in sophomore and junior years, I suffered stress injuries in my right foot; I stopped running midway through junior year. I was depressed about it and felt disconnected from my body. Instead of getting physical therapy, I just rebelled against athletics for a few years. It was during this anti-athletics phase that I got onto the school paper and met Ellen.

I returned to running only slowly during college and after, but I tended toward shorter distances. Ellen was running dozens of miles at a time on roads and racing in marathons.

Our first hike together, a month after the reunion, was a day loop of Mount Jackson and Mount Webster. Ellen drove us to Crawford Notch after I spent the night with her in Arlington, Massachusetts. We started up the trail with our dogs: my miniature poodle, Talley, and Ellen's Cavalier King Charles spaniel, Isabel. Ellen doled out dog treats every so often to motivate Isabel.

I led us past a confusing intersection, and Ellen told me I was a "goddess of the Whites." I laughed. I did not feel anything like a goddess, but I did know the White Mountains. A light snow began to fall. Clouds swirled in and out, and on the summits, they parted long enough to reveal mountainsides of browns and reds just below a white line where the snow had adhered. It was stunning. On the way down, the snow intensified, and Ellen called out, "Look at the ice balls all over the dogs' legs!"

Tackling these mountains would be difficult with a small dog, but not impossible. Tom Ryan had done it with Atticus. Isabel was special. Ellen took her on many other hikes and shared photos of Isabel staring out at distant ridges from rocky summits.

Over the next year, Ellen continued to hike the 4,000-footers when she could, often with her friend Kate, whom I'd known in high school, too. In July 2013, I led her on a trek up Lafayette, Garfield, and Galehead, a trip punctuated by rain and clouds. We capped that trip with a day hike up Mount Washington in fog. We left our dogs home for that.

The next January, Isabel suddenly got very sick and died of heart failure. She was not yet 11 years old. Ellen grieved her close canine friend.

In 2014, we talked about another trip. That August, we set out on a three-day trek that would include the Carter Range and Mount Monroe.

I packed a book I'd long thought I was supposed to understand—and never could. I wanted Ellen to help me interpret it: *Trout Fishing in America* by Richard Brautigan, published in 1967, which has been called one of the most important environmental books of all time. I hoped we could figure out why.

We set out up the Carter–Moriah Trail on a sunny July afternoon. Ellen seemed less enthusiastic than she had on earlier trips, but we enjoyed the lovely summit of Moriah and soon reached Imp Campsite.

After I'd put up the tent and made us dinner, Ellen took out the book. It's a fictional pastiche that wanders on 112 cryptic pages through suburban landscapes of Brautigan's memory. He posed the question to himself: how had he first heard about trout fishing?. And then answered it: his stepfather had talked about trout "as if they were a precious and intelligent metal."

Ellen Finnie near Carter Lake.

I asked, "Is it that trout and the freedom to fish for it epitomizes American leisure?"

Ellen read on. Brautigan described silver-colored trout by calling them "trout steel. . . . Imagine Pittsburgh. The Andrew Carnegie of trout!"

Ellen laughed helplessly, and then I started laughing, collapsing in hilarity over something we didn't understand, just as we had laughed during newspaper disasters in high school. Writing well remained as important to us as a beautiful rainbow trout. The Andrew Carnegie of words!

As the sky went deeper gray near sunset, she sat by the tent door and read on while I put some last things into the stuff sacks. According to Brautigan, what had looked like a creek tumbling off a hill actually was a wooden staircase in the forest.

We laughed again. "This must all come together to something important," I said, trying to figure out an explanation. Brautigan, a former high school newspaper writer himself, did not make it easy. His opaque style seemed to both anticipate and epitomize the countercultural moment of the late 1960s. The book wandered from humorous imaginings to satire and back. Ellen read: "Then I knocked on the creek and heard the sound of wood." *What?*

The next morning, I said, "I think maybe *Trout Fishing in America* is about pollution. It might be about the destruction of waterways." I had gathered water from the stream and was pumping it from my water bag through my old filter into a bottle as Ellen held the bottle steady.

Brautigan ended that chapter with a brief aside to the reader, called "The reply of *Trout Fishing in America*." He apologized for the weird image of a staircase taken for a stream. He said he could not handle it otherwise. He added that he had once mistaken an older woman for a trout stream.

Again we chortled. How could we help it? I loved this kind of moment with Ellen. And here in the mountains, I felt at my most relaxed, the most deep "me" I could be.

But my partner was not at ease. She was wanting to go home. She had adopted a puppy not long before, a white golden retriever named Gracie who had filled the space in her heart that was grieving the spaniel Isabel. But Gracie was still very young, and although Ellen had left the puppy in good hands, she seemed distracted with worry. Dogsickness, homesickness.

Ellen and I continued along the Carter Range. She helped me up the high ledge on North Carter that always scared me. We crossed Carter Dome and then descended the rock stairs to Carter Notch Hut, our destination that night. The next morning, we walked out Nineteen Mile Brook Trail. That afternoon, we were planning to drive over to the Ammonoosuc Ravine Trail near the Cog Railway and head up to Lakes of the Clouds Hut.

While we waited for our clothing to finish the spin cycle at the laundromat in Gorham, I took out my small notepad and suggested we make a grid of pros and cons for Ellen continuing. The list teetered toward her leaving. "I think it's the puppy," I said.

That was it. She told me she was yearning to go home and see the puppy. She also was worried that Gracie would not do well on big mountains. Because of that, this journey was not making her feel alive. It was making her feel exhausted in body and spirit.

We gathered our clean laundry, and I packed a few things for the trail. Ellen set out to drive home. First, she drove me to retrieve my car and then followed me while I drove to the Appalachia trailhead on Route 2 in Randolph. (This would be the end point of the hike I was continuing without her.) I parked there, and she drove me back past Crawford Notch and dropped me at the trailhead for the Ammonoosuc Trail to Lakes of the Clouds Hut. I waved goodbye and headed up alone.

I wanted to be the kind of person who could accept any decisions my friends made. One point of going into the mountains is learning that a mountain will not budge. My expectations cannot force a mountain to mold around me. Ellen's assumptions—her initial hopes and her altered ones—must consider the relative permanence of a pile of rocks.

"You have to be on fire to climb these mountains," I told her.

I felt that Ellen might judge herself harshly. She got in touch with me later, after writing a blog post about the puppy's needs tugging her body and heart back home. I understood, although I had never had that experience. I wondered what might have happened if I'd started climbing big mountains with big goals when my children were small. I likely would have felt my motherhood ripping into my desire to climb.

Even without puppies or babies, anyone who climbs may feel their firm summit goals unraveling about halfway through a trek—when the dreaming and planning fail to meet the realities. The weather turns bad. Someone sprains an ankle. A wrong turn makes it impossible to reach camp by dark. The quest rearranges itself into something new, strange, and even scary.

The mountains are hard enough without forcing oneself up them when the spirit flags.

I wrote to Ellen later that I understood her unsettled feelings, especially about major mountains. "If I could articulate for you just how terrified I felt when, more than three months into my journey up the Appalachian Trail, I dragged myself and my load into the Whites, that might help you see what I mean."

I assured her that she had been resilient. Tough. That whether she reached the top of a certain set of peaks or not did not matter. What mattered was that she had traversed mountains in marginal circumstances. How many women in their 50s go backpacking for the first time? In the rain?

Everything I did at Imp Campsite I'd done hundreds of times before. Ellen was doing and watching these actions for the first time. Watching me wrestle with a borrowed tent. Finding the outhouse. Spitting toothpaste into leaf duff.

During my very first camping trip in Maine, the summer I was 10, I had been terrified to use the outdoor latrine. Our counselor had dug a hole and placed the toilet paper on a branch stuck into the ground. "Take a left at the fallen tree," she said in an ominous voice that I had not found funny.

I reminded Ellen that mountains can challenge even the strongest athletes. *You think you know hard? I'll show you hard.* That was North Carter speaking. Every trip, the weather turns sour, however briefly, reminding me yet again that part of the experience is learning to move with focus and calm instead of panic and dread. Out of that, I grow.

Brautigan's veiled messages stayed in my head. Ellen analyzed the book a bit in one of her emails. "Could *Trout Fishing in America* mean, essentially, authenticity?" she wrote. Was the author playing around with truth by hiding it? Sort of both sides of "The Emperor with No Clothes"? She wrote that she thought perhaps Brautigan "plays around with what is real/authentic, by using obfuscation and meanderings," and the people who tried to say what was really happening were courageous.

She said she would never have even opened the inscrutable Brautigan if I had not asked her to read it to me. Of course, I would not have persisted with that confusing book without a reading buddy.

I had hoped to decipher Brautigan, and I wanted someone smart to bushwhack into it with me. I don't know if any of Brautigan's fans, even, could explain him. Ellen and I certainly could not. Maybe some of his readers were pretending they understood something about conservation and consumerism that wasn't actually clear. Maybe I was learning that I didn't need to understand everything.

Brautigan was *not* writing about trout fishing. He may or may not have meant to comment on pollution of waterways or deride the consumer values that swept the United States after World War II. I have never found a source that could definitively tell me what *Trout Fishing in America* means. My version of Brautigan's trout stream that turned into a wooden staircase is a cliff on a mountain that turns into a memory. On a mountain, a ledge jutting off a cliff stands firm and literal. I do not have to decipher why the cliff becomes the memory cliff once I'm home, and why the memory cliff means more to my life than the real cliff did.

Even in all the confusion, my Brautigan-like memory cliff offered the answer to the question: Was I a peakbagger? Did expectations drive my mountain legs?

Yes. Well . . . a recovering peakbagger. Assumptions don't serve one very well in an environment where the weather is cloudy more than half the time. Yet the peakbagger inside me had gotten me to that place where I could learn the big lesson: the summit itself is simply a bonus. It sounds trite, almost a universal point mountain climbers make. But the details of knowing this are a web of human emotions and bald facts, like weather and how well rested I am.

The times I did not go to the top had made me into the woman who could take Ellen camping in the rain and ask her to read out loud from Richard Brautigan.

HEALING BY DOING

My husband and I were in a bad place one summer, so we left home and went into the mountains for three days. Nat had just had another teaching contract end—the second time in fifteen months. It wasn't his fault: he worked on yearly teaching contracts at private schools, and the economy was poor just then. The old ways of coping with change had led me to a brick wall. I could not search the job listings for someone else. Hadn't three decades with him taught me not to do that? Yet I was in despair.

We both knew one thing: we could carry our stuff on our backs up to the Riga Mountain ridge on the Connecticut–Massachusetts border. We could camp.

Weighed down by loss and trying not to say the wrong thing to each other, we pulled the gear off the shelves. It'd been a while since we'd gone together;

Nat rests on Bear Mountain, July 2013.

we found to our surprise that during Nat's purge of old equipment, he'd given away our two-person tent. So we borrowed one. He dragged out an old stove he'd found somewhere—I had my doubts that it would be reliable, but I have always trusted him with the stove. I plotted our route, as I had been doing for many years; he trusted me to do that. He cleaned the water filter. I packed the food. We were used to letting each other do those things.

Of all the things he and I had done together—move five times, raise children, look for work, sit by each other's sickbeds—backpacking was the one we often did in silence. We had hiked thousands of miles together. I had hiked perhaps a thousand more without him. Of all the places we could start healing, the mountains seemed the obvious choice.

It's one thing to feel love, even selfless love, but sometimes in life, you have to just shut up and walk. Now we would do again what we once had loved to do together. So, we parked the car and buried the keys in my pack. Talley, our miniature poodle, sniffed the ground, and we began climbing the steep slope. The rocks were soaked from weeks of downpours. Clouds of mosquitoes followed us. All afternoon I breathed in rhythm with Nat's trudging. We camped in a shelter down the ridge from a group of orphan boys in a state wilderness program. They ran over to meet Talley as their leaders stirred huge pots of stew.

The next morning, as I struggled with my big pack, Nat waded in with suggestions on how to load it. I turned toward him, fuming. "I cannot concentrate when you interrupt me like this!" I was yelling.

He backed away. I hyperventilated into my stuff sacks. A few minutes went by. I punched my clothing bag into the bottom of the pack. The lunch bag next. The heavier stove in its padding went in the part of the pack that would rest close to my back. As Nat had taught me.

I knew he did not deserve my anger. I went over to him and said, "I'm sorry."

"You don't need to apologize," he said.

"Yes, I do," I said. We had fallen into one of our old habits: trying to meet each other halfway and going farther than that. A marriage counselor once told us that part of our problem was we were *too* solicitous. However, out there on the ridge, there was no time or proper place to keep up this kind of negotiation. We had to start walking. So we scrambled up to Mount Everett and across the wet rocks of Mount Race. Nat's muscular legs in their baggy gaiters faded in and out of fog. He picked some blueberries for me at lunch. Talley climbed so strongly over the slippery treadway that Nat called her the sure-footed mountain goat. The sun began to beam through the mist.

As I walked through the afternoon, it came to me: *Be patient. Become the woman you can be.*

Our second night out, we met some wonderful young hikers—some thru-hiking the Appalachian Trail—and a ridge-runner, a 26-year-old woman who rallied about six of us to carry an improperly moved picnic table back to where it belonged. We gathered water, lit the stove, set up the tent, and listened to each other's trail stories.

The peace of chores, which had eluded me in our little house, settled in. Much later, as my husband and my dog slept soundly next to me, I sat up and pulled out my headlamp and notebook. As I always do when camping, I scribbled down some notes (notes that help me write this now). Late at night, I could think about how easily we cooperated out here. I could picture Nat earlier that day, a man I had not seen in a long time—wise, funny, with a bandanna hanging around his ears and a maroon baseball cap on his head.

Nat hiking, as Talley follows.

On the third day, we slid over the slick, worn rocks of the old mountains. The footing was more dangerous than on wet granite, and I knew that the rocks didn't care. Rocks are like problems that won't budge. But when you look closely, you realize that both contain cracks and handholds. For Nat and me, the future remained hidden. But I could see a way to get to it.

For weeks after we went home, when I closed my eyes, I would see the wet boulders, leaf duff, mud, streams, and cairns. I knew that I could learn to get through and around them in a way that makes sense, in the right time. The trip had marked the climb up from a low point. The way out would not take us as long as I had feared.

Nat and I went on to finish the northern stretches of the Long Trail. We trudged up to open summits, set up camp, shared food, and talked. A 10-year-old girl hiking the whole trail with her father nicknamed us Mr. and Mrs. Ion: the negative force and the positive force. Mr. Ion and I are two pilgrims on the same long journey.

FORWARD: A FOUR-SEASON ALMANAC
OF WILDERNESS LESSONS

My mountain life has created an almanac for the rest of my life. Mountains inhabit the self long after the body has inhabited the mountains. Here I lay out what I've learned in my mountain life, expressed as a guide to living through the four seasons in New England.

Winter: Prepare. Rest.

I was not a great planner before I started backpacking. I still prefer working to a deadline and motivating myself with the pressure of limited time. But preparation is important. Planning a project step by step, and executing it step by step, shows maturity. Backpacking is where I learned this. For days before I leave for a mountain trip, I gather and pack everything I need. I make lists. If I forget something, I will be stuck without that thing. In civilized life, I often wait too long to start preparing—for example, shoving food into a bag when I should be leaving for the train station. For a backpacking trip, I would have packed that food the night before. I am still learning to follow mountain lessons at home.

In winter, where I live, the weather often determines whether you can even get into your car. In a broader sense, winter determines what I won't do. I won't do as much running around on errands in the cold and dark. In winter, I will spend more time indoors thinking and planning for the future. Terry Tempest Williams once told an interviewer that a bear in winter provides a model for women, because after a long hibernation in fall and winter, she comes out with babies. "The bear becomes our mentor. We must journey out, so that we might journey in."[1]

---

1 Michael Austin, *Voice in the Wilderness: Conversations with Terry Tempest Williams*, Kindle edition (Utah State University Press, 2006), page 28.

A tree grows around a boulder in Canfield Woods, Deep River, Connecticut.

Spring: Feed what needs feeding.

In the mountains, I have learned to love and honor my physical self. I have learned that food is life. That a woman should never deprive herself of food on the basis of an imagined ideal appearance. I have learned that my body is made for moving, lifting and carrying, and helping others. I have learned never to hate my physical appearance but to appreciate all the ways my body has taken me to remote places.

Summer: Savor the moment but know my limits.

Summer is the high season in New England for moving through mountains. I move fast, if I want, through wild places, but I never do it at the risk of not getting out alive.

Study the plants and animals. Understand, if possible, where they live and how they move. Respect their homes and keep my voice quiet. Summer is the blooming of everything in a short time in New England. Appreciate its temporality.

Fall: Take in the harvest of knowledge.

Understand that humans are naturally communal beings. Nurture human relationships. Think about what to say before saying it. I've made mistakes in my friendships and relationships, but I've tried to recognize them and move forward in positive ways. Mountain trips also have drawn me closer to the people who have walked with me. They have helped me care for others.

On so many mountain trips I've thought, *I'm just getting started with these partners. I'm just getting started exploring this ridge. When I come back, I'll check out that side trail to that other overlook. I love the way the wind ripples that stunted spruce. I'll be back. I will see that again.*

But any of these moments could be the last time I'm walking on that trail in that way. The last time alone. The last time with beloved partners. The last time my poodle, Talley, zigzags up that boulder. The last time I come up that particular trail.

Just as often, I know that many years of exploring backcountry places await.

These times on the mountains are like jewels. Every time I'm on a mountain now, I think, *This could be the last time. You may never be back here. Savor it.* I also think, *I hope I'll be back here again.*

The sign that the mountains have done their work is when the mountains stay inside after I've left.

Frost on a red spruce on the Willey Range Trail in New Hampshire's White Mountains.

ACKNOWLEDGMENTS

I would like to thank all the people who have walked through the mountains and life with me. Nat Eddy, Phil Lodine, and Cay Lodine, have been companions on the Appalachian Trail and through so much else. Nat's and my daughters, Elizabeth Eddy and Annie Spencer-Eddy Levine, walked bravely with me on dozens of uncomfortable and sometimes sensational adventures from very young ages. Even as tiny children, they were wise and selfless, thinking first of their mother in ways that still amaze me.

Thank you, Summit New England crew, for your competitive zeal and hilarity: Nat, Skip Weisenburger, Spyros Barres, Maggie Jones, Brian Chidley, Tom Beattie, the late Ray Cherenzia, Steve Fagin, Phil Plouffe, and our driver and team doctor, Bob Graham.

I owe deep thanks to Bob Fales and Zoe Fales, with whom I followed ridges in the Adirondacks, Maine, and White Mountains. Thank you for taking care of each other and watching out for me. Thanks to Leigh Weisenburger Albert, a wonderful companion on more than a few Presidential Range traverses. Thanks to Peter Jonas and Kit Wang, companions on my first big mountain trip.

Skip Weisenburger made mountains fun and expanded joy no matter who was in the group; thank you for your big heart, humor, loyalty, gourmet food, and photography. Steve Fagin, a trusted colleague in journalism for many years, and Tom Fagin, shared the trails with humor and patience.

Ellen Finnie brought a fresh sense of discovery and bravery to three White Mountains hikes. I can't think of a better person with whom to puzzle over Richard Brautigan.

Martha Lyon and I have shared life's transitions, pleasures, sorrows, and many mountains since we were in college. Thanks, Martha, for keeping me honest in writing and hiking.

Jenifer McShane has believed in many of my writing projects and understood me like a sister for many years. Thank you, Jen. Thanks also to Lynn Cochrane, who understands dreams and ambitions. For exploration of backcountry places going back many years, I thank my siblings, Robert H. Woodside, J. Stephen Woodside, John T. Woodside, and Anne Woodside Gribbins; my brother-in-law Malcolm Meldahl, my late sister-in-law Nell Eddy Meldahl; my brother-in-law and sister-in-law David Eddy and Allison Taylor; my sister-in-law and brother-in-law Maria Tjeltveit and Alan Tjeltveit; and many other family members. I love you all.

Many writer colleagues and workshop leaders read drafts of pieces that went into this book. All of them improved my words and helped me discern my points: Nell Lake, Tim Bascom, Karen Weintraub, Kathleen Burge, Farah Stockman, Karen Brown, Pagan Kennedy, Judy Rakowsky, Mark Kramer, Dan Grossman, Cynthia Anderson, Gregory Norris, Roxanne Dent, Karen Dent, Marymartha Bell, Judi Calhoun, and other members of the Berlin, New Hampshire Writers.

To Appalachian Mountain Club Senior Books Editor Timothy Mudie, thank you for taking on this book and guiding its evolution to a full volume whose stories connect. Thanks to Senior Production Manager Abigail Coyle for top-notch guidance with a hillock of photos.

Finally, for lodging and hospitality during fair and stormy mountain weather in Randolph, New Hampshire, I thank John Phinney, Harriet Phinney, and Jennifer and the late John Scarinza.

Finally, thanks to so many members of St. John's Episcopal Church, especially Allison Fresher and the Rev. Kate Wesch.

ABOUT THE AUTHOR

CHRISTINE WOODSIDE is a writer, historian, and editor. Her previous book is *Libertarians on the Prairie: Laura Ingalls Wilder, Rose Wilder Lane, and the Making of the Little House Books*. She is the editor-in-chief of *Appalachia*, the journal of the Appalachian Mountain Club. She was editor of the adventure anthology *No Limits But the Sky: The Best Mountaineering Stories from* Appalachia *Journal* and *New Wilderness Voices: Collected Essays from the Waterman Fund Contest*, a book of work by emerging writers. She lives in Deep River, Connecticut.

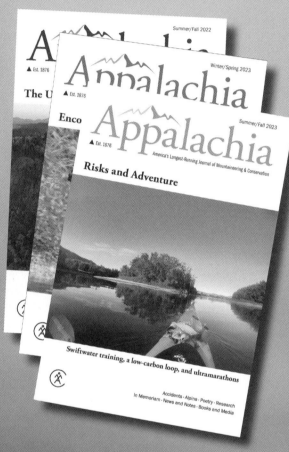